FERRARI
TESTAROSSA

Autofolio

TESTAROSSA

PHILIP PORTER

Autofolio

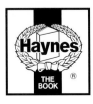

A **FOULIS** Motoring Book

First Published 1990

© Haynes Publishing Group 1990

Published by: Haynes Publishing Group
Sparkford, Nr Yeovil, Somerset BA22 7JJ

Haynes Publications Inc.
861 Lawrence Drive, Newbury Park,
California 91320, USA

British Library Cataloguing in Publication Data
Porter, Philip
    Ferrari Testarossa autofolio.
    1. Ferrari Testarossa cars
    I. Title
    629.2222
ISBN 0-85429-734-0

Library of Congress catalog card number 90-83287

Series Photographer: David Sparrow
Editor: Mansur Darlington
Book design: Camway Autographics
Printed in England by: J.H. Haynes & Co. Ltd
Typeset in: 9/11pt Frontiera light roman

CONTENTS

Autofolio

There is an undeniable excitement about the Ferrari marque. It is intoxicating to any enthusiast so, when I was asked to write the first book in this new series, I had little hesitation in choosing the Testarossa from the shortlist provided.

Most of my motoring books have been on Jaguar so I cannot, on the face of it, claim to be qualified to write a Ferrari book! On the other hand, it can be argued that I am not partisan, and maybe I can be dispassionate enough to sift facts from myth, reality from legend.

In assisting with formulating the structure for the series of books of which this is one, I talked to a number of enthusiasts to seek their ideas and ascertain what they might want of a book devoted to one particular model. One interesting idea emerged, which we have incorporated, and that is to include the comments of a leading specialist in the field, both upon the car and what they are like to work on. In this instance Bob Houghton was the obvious choice. His amazing workshop is full of such cars as GTOs, the sports racing 512s, Formula One Ferraris et al. I am grateful to Bob for taking the time to share a little of his vast experience and expertise.

The other ingredient, which we felt to be vital, was a driving feature; not as a 'test' in the conventional sense but to put you in the driving seat gaining the impressions that you might gain as an owner. To do this, we decided upon the medium of a back-to-back comparison with another car chosen as suitable counterpoint to the main subject car. Here we were extremely fortunate to have the whole-hearted co-operation of Paul Lennon and John Young, owners respectively of the Testarossa and Daytona featured. I cannot thank them enough for all their help and patience.

Wishing to talk to some owners, I attended a Ferrari gathering and was particularly fortunate to meet John Sager and Richard Downey, coincidentally both over from New Zealand to collect their Testarossas and run them for a while in the UK. I think their comments are especially revealing and make good reading.

That David 'Watch the Birdie' Sparrow has done superbly is evidenced by the high standard of the photography. Apart from the pleasure of working with such a professional, David has a great sense of humour and we had a lot of fun.

I would like to thank the editors of the various journals quoted from, for kind permission to do so.

I always enjoy working with Mansur Darlington, the Managing Editor of G.T.Foulis, and this project has been no exception. As ever, I am grateful to him for his wise counsel and good humour.

Finally thanks are due to Mark Konig at Maranello Concessionaires for supplying the photo of the original Testa Rossa.

Philip Porter

As with almost every Ferrari, the creation of the Testarossa was heavily influenced by the racing cars from the same stable, adapting and using the technology learnt therefrom. But this was no harsh, thinly disguised racer. The sophisticated Testarossa was something of a departure for Ferrari and reflected the involvement of Fiat and the lure of the vast potential of the American market.

The heritage is famed and unquestionable. Ferrari have competed in Formula One longer than every other team. From the 125's debut in May 1947, Ferraris have won over 5000 races, including more than 90 victories in Formula One, 14 World titles for Makes, taken nine wins at both Le Mans and the Targa Florio, one less in the Mille Miglia and taken drivers to the Formula One World Championship no less than nine times. It is hardly surprising that the road cars have such a unique image and aura.

But these intangible qualities are not due solely to the reflected glory gained from such competitive success. Most of the road cars have deserved acclaim in their own right. Indeed, all have benefited in some way from the racing developments and some have been more closely inspired by racing trends than others. Especially with regard to its engine, the modern Testarossa is an excellent example of a production Ferrari descended from the racing machines.

The company was, of course, created by the late Enzo Ferrari who, though turned ninety, was still involved in 'his' firm right up to the time of his death.

By many accounts, he was not an easy man to work for or with, as is so often the case with strong personalities who know precisely what they want. Nevertheless he achieved such a great deal that he had acquired a unique position in the motoring world. In his later years the man was surrounded by a hallowed aura such that, in 1988, even the Pope visited this shrine of the sporting motor car.

Right from the very start, when production commenced in 1947, Ferrari always favoured twelve-cylinder cars, and in particular V12s. Characteristically, Ferrari was oblivious to trends when he introduced a V12 in his first offering. Though such engines had been employed in the more affluent and indulgent pre-war years, post-war strictures dictated simpler configurations – for most.

Today it is not so easy to appreciate how bold and brave a step this must have been in 1947. The V12 has been reborn in more recent years, a trend that commenced with Lamborghini in 1964 but which received a considerable fillip when Jaguar introduced their relatively 'mass production' V12, first in the ageing E-type in 1971, and then in the XJ12 saloon. In the eighties we had BMW following suit with Mercedes-Benz dangerously not so far behind. Such events have, ironically, caused Jaguar to abandon plans to drop their engine, whose early life unhappily coincided with the fuel crisis of the seventies and the new-found interest in petrol consumption.

Such mundane considerations never seem to have affected Ferrari. Indeed their market was comparatively so small that they could afford to assume what almost amounts to an arrogance, which has only served to further heighten the mystique surrounding the Italian make.

Twelve cylinder engines have formed the basis of most Ferraris ever since Gioacchino Columbo designed the first generation of V12s in 1946/7. From this beginning a whole variety of engines was sired. The first had a capacity of 1497 cc, with the two banks of cylinders inclined at 60 degrees and a bore and stroke of 55.0 x 52.5 mm. Within months a larger, 1902 cc, engine was built for the newly planned Formula Two racing category by increasing the bore and stroke to 59.0 x 58.8 mm. From there onwards the bore diameter was gradually increased with the stroke remaining constant to provide a variety of increasing engine sizes, always designated by the capacity in cubic centimetres of one single cylinder.

Columbo left in 1949 and was replaced by Aurelio Lampredi, who designed a new larger V12 using many of the features first seen in Columbo's version but with bore centre spacings of 108 mm, thereby allowing greater overall cubic capacities. This new engine, which

220/240 bhp, and in competition form when power was raised to 260/295 bhp. The 250s were raced most successfully by drivers such as de Portago, Gendebien, Bianchi, Mairesse, Parkes and Moss, the last-named winning the Tourist Trophy on two occasions in such a

was designed with the 4½-litre unsupercharged Formula One limit in mind, was known as the 'long block', being 102 mm (4 in) longer. Both engines would continue to be used in ever more developed forms and various sizes for many years to come.

The first model to be produced in any real quantity was the 250, which appeared in 1956 but would be seen in a variety of body styles. Indeed until the following year, annual production did not reach three figures and total cumulative production did not reach four figures until 1960. Production in the first ten years averaged only about a car a week with the graph showing a steady rise from the early days to the present, with the just the occasional slight dip.

The classic 250GT Berlinetta SWB (short wheelbase) was produced in road-going form, whence the 3-litre triple Weber carburetted short-block V12 developed

machine. The significance of the 250GT is that it was the last Ferrari that was really designed for both road use and racing.

Fearing greater competition from the new E-type Jaguars and from Aston Martin, Ferrari ordered his engineers to design a new car. This decision was given greater impetus by the fact that the CSI, the organising body of motor sport, announced in 1961 that, from the following year, the World Sports Car Championship would be run for GT cars. The 250 engine was retained but for the first time the Ferrari designers paid serious attention to aerodynamics. The result was that most charismatic of cars, the GTO (O for Omologati).

The GTO was very definitely a competition car, as you quickly discover when you ride in one today, and so, with this splitting of the roles, a new, more sophisticated road car was needed. The 250GT

Even on a grey day, this blue-blooded, redhead turns young enthusiasts green with envy, and passengers' knuckles white.

Reflecting the growth of the company and their desire to satisfy a larger market, the launch of the Testarossa by Ferrari was a quite different occasion than the previous rather low-key affairs, held at the Cavallino restaurant in Maranello.

A Ritzy, show business atmosphere was created at the famous Lido in the Champs Elysées, Paris. Here, in the late afternoon of 2 October 1984 before the opening of the France's motor show, the Paris Salon, the car was launched to the European Press.

As the champagne corks popped and the nectar flowed in abundant quantities, the Testarossa was revealed by its rising out of the floor. Many of the leading journalists in Europe were present and they were all invited to dine before being entertained by the famous floor show. Scantily clad redheads (what else) in thigh-length red and black boots and a head gear that resembled the splayed ends of a stripped flex, were photographed with the vivid new automotive redhead.

In the States the North American dealers had already had a preview when, with the aid of parachutists, the car was shown to them at the Imola racing circuit on 25 September.

Autofolio

Berlinetta Lusso (Luxury), with a particularly beautiful body by Pininfarina, was the answer. This in turn was replaced towards the end of 1964 by the 275GTB, which many consider to have been Ferrari's finest front-engined car, particularly in later form. Surprisingly, the famous GTO had been a comparatively conservative design retaining a live rear axle, but the 275GTB adopted independent rear suspension. The gearbox was of the transaxle variety and, as denoted by the type number, the engine capacity had now been increased to $3\frac{1}{4}$-litres (3285 cc).

Whilst the GTOs were enjoying a most successful international racing career in the GT class, the front-engined Testa Rossas were being similarly successful in the even more prestigious Prototype class. Various British manufacturers, however, notably Cooper and

Lotus, were showing the effectiveness of a mid-engined configuration and Ferrari followed suit with their Formula Two cars in 1960 and Formula One cars in their all-conquering 1961 year. It is, therefore, not surprising that a prototype sports car was also built along similar lines. The 246SP had its 2.4-litre four-cam V6 mounted amidships with a transaxle bolted to the rear of the power unit. In 1963 Ferrari introduced the V12 mid-engined 250P and, with it, won at Sebring, the Nurburgring and Le Mans. At the same time, the GTO was succeeded by the closed mid-engined 250LM, though this time Ferrari failed to convince the FIA that this GT was based on the production cars or that he had serious intentions of building 100. Thus the 250LM could not run in the GT class. These cars, however, were a pointer to future Ferrari road cars.

The 275GTB was introduced, as mentioned, in 1964, given a longer nose a year later and four cams a year after that, which had the effect of upping the power to 300 bhp. Ferrari continued to produce a number of other models apart from those specifically mentioned including the 4-litre 330s but, in late 1967, a new model appeared that was a departure for Ferrari in more ways than one It was smaller, less costly and mid-engined. The Dino, as it was known, was produced, most significantly, in conjunction with Fiat and was a great success.

However, Ferrari have traditionally adopted a conservative approach to modern developments on their production cars and thus the 275GTB/4 was replaced, not by a mid-engined car, but by Ferrari's final manifestation of the front-engined supercar. Ferrari were being typically cautious, for their precocious rivals, Lamborghini, had introduced the transverse mid-engined 4-litre V12 Miura at Turin in 1965.

The new Ferrari model, the 365GTB/4, also known as the Daytona, was introduced in 1968. Like so many Ferraris, the car's greatest merit lay in its engine. The car had a conventional chassis but the V12 engine was once more enlarged, to 4390 cc, and like its predecessor had the sophistication of four overhead camshafts. With its six twin-choke carburettors, the output was an impressive 352 bhp which powered the car to a genuine 175 mph and enabled it to reach 60 mph from rest in 5.8 seconds.

A completely new concept for Ferrari's flagship model was shown in 1971 and available from 1973,

for at last Ferrari had introduced a mid-engined supercar. But this was not all that was new about the 365GT4/BB. As usual, the road car incorporated a development first seen on the racing cars. The traditional, almost mandatory, V12 gave way to a different formation, still retaining twelve cylinders, but horizontally opposed at 180 degrees.

Ferrari were certainly not the first to employ such a concept and, indeed, the Alfa Romeo 512 and Cisitalia of earlier times had used horizontally opposed engines, but Ferrari were the first to race with such a configuration.

In late 1963 Enzo Ferrari had shown the motoring press two new Grand Prix engines of great significance. The first was a V8, which would power John Surtees to his World Championship in 1964, and the other a flat-12. The latter had been designed by Mauro Forghieri, a young man who had only joined the company in 1960 but who was destined to make a great name for himself in Formula One and later become Technical Director.

The new 1½-litre flat-12 was fitted in a similar chassis to the V8, which incidentally was Ferrari's first semi-monocoque, and run alongside the more conventional eight-cylinder car. The flat-12, known as the 1512F1 and also as the 512F1, was first used in practice in September 1964 at the Italian Grand Prix. It was not run in the race but made its debut a month later at Watkins Glen. The car continued to be raced alongside the V8 car in 1965.

The concept reappeared in 2-litre form fitted to the 212E Montagna which Peter Schetty used to dominate the European Mountain Championship in 1969. Around this time Forghieri designed a new Formula One car, the 312B, which was based around his 3-litre flat-12. Though not initially successful, the chassis and suspension were gradually revised through a succession of models throughout the decade. The early disappointment gave way to emphatic success and flat-12s carried Niki Lauda to the World Championship in 1975 and 1977, and Jody Scheckter to his two years later. The engine was not superseded until the arrival of the 'turbo era'.

Back in 1971 the same engine was fitted into a sports racing car, the 312PB, and run for an experimental season in readiness for the new 3-litre limit to be imposed in 1972. The result was total domination in 1972 with victory in all ten rounds of the championship plus two non-championship events. After a less successful following year, Ferrari retired

Autofolio

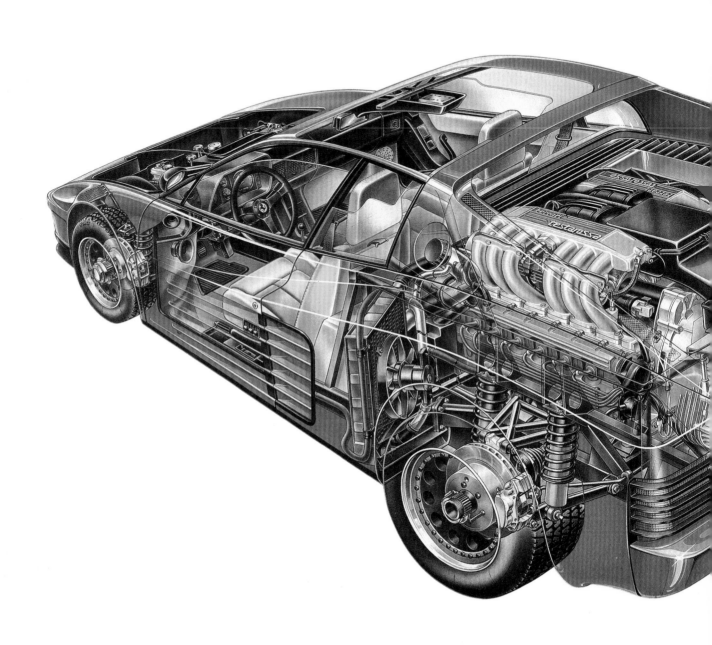

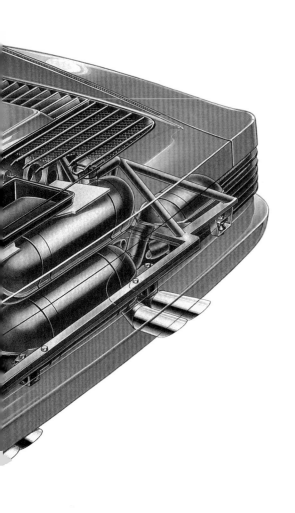

The name Testa Rossa literally means Red Head and was first used by Ferrari in 1956. It is not some reference to an Italian beauty of the human species, but rather was inspired by the striking crackle finish red cam covers which embellished the Ferrari competition engine of the time.

Though first used in 1956, the name has come to be associated with the famous Testa Rossas, the 3-litre sports racing machines of 1958 onwards. With Ferrari and Maserati producing ever larger engines to try and match the slippery D-type Jaguars, the governing body decided to impose, from the beginning of '58, a three litre limit in an effort to curb power. Ferrari adopted the faithful Columbo V12 engine and the body, by Scaglietti, was vaguely reminiscent of a catamaran with its pontoon-like wings. Chief Engineer, Carlo Chiti, decided to concentrate on reliability rather than ultimate power, a wise compromise for the long distance races that dominated the sports racing calendar. Indeed the car broke no new ground and was conservatively conventional, eschewing monocoque construction and disc brakes which Jaguar had used so successfullly on the high speed circuits.

Jaguar, however, had been seriously interested in winning only Le Mans whereas Ferrari, one suspects, was more interested in winning the overall championship. The Testa Rossa was a supremely well-sorted design that could cope well with a wide variety of circuits including the slower, twisty ones. Also, like every Ferrari, the car's great quality was its engine. Whereas Jaguar had to reduce the size of their 3.8-litre six-cylinder engines, with disastrous results, Ferrari already had a 3-litre on the stocks and furthermore had great experience of the engine.

The Jaguar factory had already retired, leaving the private entrants to battle gamely on with the ageing D-types, Maserati had decided to stand down for a while and Aston Martin were working on a new car, the DBR1. Stirling Moss showed his mastery in one of the last named cars at the uniquely challenging Nürburging, but otherwise the Testa Rossas dominated, winning all the other rounds in which they competed, including Le Mans where no less than 10 examples took part.

Gradual developments included the fitting of de Dion rear suspension, a five-speed transaxle transmission, revised bodywork and, finally, disc brakes. However, Aston Martin turned the tables on their Italian rivals in 1959 and took the championship with the Testa Rossas being afflicted by particularly poor reliability.

For the 1960 season the Testa Rossas were given independent rear suspension, but the season began badly with a number of retirements. Prestige was salvaged at Le Mans however, when Olivier Gendebien and Paul Frere headed a Testa Rossa 1-2 in appalling conditions.

The 1961 season saw the curious shark-nosed Ferrari dominate the new $1\frac{1}{2}$-litre Formula One and the same frontal styling favoured by Carlo Chiti was adopted on the rebodied Testa Rossas. The rejuvenated cars won three of the five championship rounds, against strong opposition from the very fast but frail 'birdcage' Maseratis, and the sucesses included yet another Le Mans victory.

The model was then effectively retired but one example, fitted with an enlarged, 4-litre unit, was entered by the works for the French classic in 1962.

As a fitting climax to a great career, the Testa Rossa won and the now-hallowed name entered the history books to be used no more – until, that is, 1984 when the name was resurrected as the Testarossa.

An evocative name to conjure with, the new Testarossa had a great reputation to live up to.

from sports car racing and sadly have not returned.

When planning the new road going supercar to replace the Daytona, there was no question that it must be mid-engined. It was also inconceivable to imagine a Ferrari flagship without a twelve-cylinder engine, but the flat-12 configuration offered itself, not only as a proven layout in competition, but also as having certain practical advantages. The perennial

sump lubrication and a toothed belt drive to the four overhead cams. Power output was stated to be 344 bhp at 7000 rpm, with the four Weber carburettors fitted, and this power was transmitted through the five-speed integral gearbox. Suspension was independent and by double wishbones and coil springs all round. Though 0.4 sec faster to 60 mph, the mid-engined car was actually fractionally slower on top speed, at 173 mph, though admittedly this is splitting hairs.

The new car was clothed in a body styled, as usual, by Pininfarina, and was, in a sense, a scaled-up version of the little 246 Dino, yet this enlarging worked superbly well and resulted in what must surely be one of the classic body designs of all time. It was catalogued as the 365GT4/BB – a 4.4-litre engined GT car with four cams and Berlinetta bodywork with Boxer engine configuration. The term 'boxer' refers to the pistons of the flat engine working akin to boxers punching!

With American Federal regulations beginning to bite and influence other countries to pursue similar bureaucratic meddling in car design and specification, it was necessary to increase the Boxer's engine capacity, in 1976, to maintain a respectable power output and meet new emission and noise standards. Thus the engine was enlarged to 4942 cc. Power was actually reduced, at 340 bhp, but torque was improved. Dry sumping was once more adopted, a small chin spoiler was added to reduce lift, and the same tyres were no longer used all round, being of nine inch width at the rear, as opposed to the 7 3/4 inch wide rubber employed at the sharp end. The new model was simply known as the 512BB.

In 1981 that designation sprouted an 'i' which indicated that the car was now fitted with fuel injection. The 512BBi used the Bosch K-Jetronic system which enabled the engineers to meet the ever more challenging emission controls. Injection did not increase the power output but had the beneficial effect of improving flexibility and smoothness.

Sophistication, it seems, was becoming the name of the game, even for Ferrari, rather than outright power which was the god in former times. Could Ferrari combine sophistication and practicality with sensuous excitement amid all the stifling regulations of the eighties? That was the challenge to be faced in creating the Boxer's successor.

The Fantuzzi-bodied Testa Rossa 250 '0776' with which Ferrari won the 1959 Sebring 12-Hours. These cars achieved an enviable record over a surprisingly long period and did a good deal to further the Ferrari legend.

problem faced by designers of mid-engined cars is one of where to site the luggage area and the lack of available space. The low, sloping nose of such a car was pretty full of radiator and spare wheel, which effectively precluded the use of this area. The Dino and Miura had addressed the problem by mounting their engines east/west, and the Lotus Esprit engine was considerably shorter having only a third of the number of cylinders.

Instead of siting the gearbox and final drive behind the engine, it was realised that the low overall height of the 'flat' engine would allow the gearbox to be sited under the engine thus foreshortening the whole package and allowing the 'boot' to be positioned in its conventional situation. The engine was built to the same 4.4-litre size as the Daytona and this allowed certain parts, including pistons, to be carried over. Unlike the Daytona, the new engine would have wet-

DESIGN AND DEVELOPMENT

The American Federal regulations of the nineteen seventies, which so disastrously affected so many of the world's great cars and killed so many concepts, made no great difference to Ferrari for the simple reason that he ignored them. Ferrari, characteristically, chose not to compromise his ideals and thus, offficially, no twelve-cylinder Ferraris were sold in the States in the seventies.

This was for two reasons. First, the Boxer engine could not easily meet the US exhaust emission regulations and, secondly, Ferrari was not prepared, it is to be thanked, to ruin the beautiful Berlinetta Boxer body by the adoption of the impact resisting bumpers which have so adversely affected many a pure line but

which were decreed by these infamous regulations.

Whether a decline in the European market influenced a change of heart is not clear but from the outset the Testarossa was designed with the large and lucrative US market in mind.

The Testarossa did not set out to be a revolutionary new design but rather to be an updating and refining of the Boxer package. One very definite criticism of the Boxer, from the point of view of practicality, was the decidedly mean amount of luggage space provided, with the obvious constraints that that placed upon touring. This was one important reason for a fundamental decision to move the radiator from the front of the car. Instead a pair would

The Ferrari Berlinetta Boxer, first in 365GT4/BB form and later in BB512 guise, introduced the Ferrari flagship model to the now almost mandatory mid-engined configuration, and was a car of rare beauty.

be mounted amidships, with one on each side, along the lines of single-seater practice. First seen on the Lotus 72 Grand Prix car in 1970, Ferrari adopted the idea for its 1973 Formula One 312B3, also nicknamed the 'snowplough'!

Resiting the radiators also had the beneficial effect of concentrating more weight in the centre of the car, with its obvious benefits to handling, and furthermore the aerodynamics would benefit from the fact that radiator apertures were no longer needed in the nose area. Yet another advantage was the fact that the radiators would now be adjacent to the engine and thus would be overcome one of the inherent disadvantages of a mid-engined car with front-mounted radiator, namely the piping of hot water to and fro through the entire length of the car including the cockpit.

Some Ferrari devotees have expressed the view that the Boxer was under-tyred. The extra width necessitated by the side-mounted radiators gave the Testarossa the necessary bodywork spread to house considerably wider rear tyres. All this, however, did lead inevitably to a wider car and that has not been to everyone's liking. The Testarossa is a large car and in all respects exceeds the dimensions of its predecessor: it is longer, has a greater wheelbase, is considerably wider and even fractionally higher.

The significance of the repositioning of the radiators cannot be overstressed, for in other respects the design of the Testarossa broke no new ground and was comparatively conservative. The newly positioned radiators not only gave the advantages outlined above, but they largely dictated the shape of the car. Indeed Sergio Pininfarina, whose legendary styling studio was retained by Ferrari to design the new model, has gone on record as stating that, 'this characteristic, more than any other, influenced the shape of the car and its personality'.

Ferrari laid down certain basic criteria, such as wheelbase, track, engine position, and passenger and luggage area minima. First thoughts did not embrace the mid-radiator layout and the early sketches showed a strong Boxer influence. This design featured a large rear window which followed the falling roof line to the tail and curved down to meet the tops of the wheel arches. A forward sloping panel rose from the wing line to the roof giving the impression of a roll-over bar. At the front the pointed nose wore a chin spoiler and a NACA duct ahead of the front wheel centre-line. The bottom sill line was curved akin to previous Pininfarina styling exercises and the one-off Aston Martin Bulldog. At the rear, the lights were very neatly enshrouded by the body and partially hidden by a series of horizontal slats. In a revised form this last feature would be retained for the final version.

This first styling exercise looks a neat and stylish solution but like many a sketch may not have been entirely practical. Matters changed direction, however, when Ferrari decided upon the mid-mounted radiators and Pininfarina had the challenge of incorporating this feature into their style. The next rendering did not differ greatly but one can see a very much larger air scoop behind the door for obvious reasons. At this

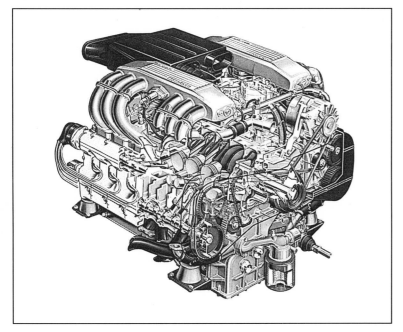

stage, this was merely a traditional open vent without adornment. The apparent roll-over hoop was visually stressed by raising it fractionally above the roofline, which can hardly have helped the drag factor, though would have assisted downforce.

For aerodynamic reasons, this design featured a form of rear wing. Ferrari displayed their conservative approach when they rejected this as being too radical and not the Ferrari way of doing things – or perhaps they felt that their traditional clientele might consider this a little too flamboyant. Whatever the reason, it is a little ironic that the F40 employs just such a device.

The next design drawn by the Pininfarina stylists adopted a notable Testarossa characteristic. Namely, as the dramatic and accentuated rear wing line swept up from the door, over the wide rear wheels and levelled, the cockpit roof line tapered as it fell away and as the body width increased. This served to give a distinctive styling feature, accentuate the width of the car and was aerodynamically efficient giving good negative lift. The rear wing line, which commenced as far forward as the door front edge, did so in the shape of what appeared to be an enormous NACA duct. The area behind the cockpit was still enclosed by a sloping rear window, though this was now approximately square and no longer 'folded' down to meet the wing line as in an earlier exercise. The rear lights, whilst still being in a recessed area and 'guarded' by a grille, now wrapped around at the corners and were close to the final design.

The next sketches were very close to the eventual car. One can see the first suggestion of the slatted side grilles for the radiator intakes. The nose displays a long overhang with a blunt leading edge in which are situated certain lights and the flatter bonnet line blends into the similarly angled windscreen to give a clean wedge shape.

That the car should end up wedge-shaped is hardly surprising when you consider that the style was dictated by a specification that included a mid-mounted engine, mid-radiators and wide rear tyres, plus the search for a shape that would allow, and be stable at, speeds in the region of 180 mph (300 kph). With the competition to build supercars with ever higher top speeds, surely for kudos rather than use, style, it seems, must become more and more subservient to aerodynamics as time passes.

At this stage it was undecided whether to retain a sloping rear window or resort to a vertical window and flat engine cover. Though the former might have been

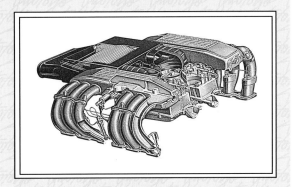

Giovanni Battista Razelli, Ferrari's managing director, stated in 1986 that the V12 would live on but that the flat-12 would not. The latter would be replaced in the early nineties. The reasons expressed were that the engine was large, bulky, heavy, difficult to service and, due to the final drive being positioned under the engine, this configuration dictated an undesirably high centre of gravity. He stated that the V12 was more practical and could be placed lower in the chassis. These were the hard, objective reasons given, but one cannot help wondering if a little Italian emotion played a part in their decision.

In 1988 he stated that Testarossa production was running at 1000 per annum, with total output up to the 4000 level. He was quoted in an interview with Gavin Green, Editor of Car, as saying that, 'there are no specific plans for the Testarossa replacement. The car is doing very well and it is still quite new.'

Interestingly, the late Enzo Ferrari stated, in his last years, that today's customer is more interested in acceleration than top speed, and this would colour future thinking.

Performance

Acceleration

mph	Car and Driver	Road & Track	Motor	Autocar
0-30	1.9	1.9	2.2	2.6
0-40	2.6	2.6	–	3.4
0-50	3.5	3.4	4.2	4.3
0-60	5.0	5.0	5.3	5.8
0-70	6.2	6.2	6.6	7.1
0-80	7.7	7.5	8.4	8.8
0-90	9.8	9.6	–	10.6
0-100	12.0	11.2	12.2	12.7
0-110	15.3	14.3	14.9	15.5
0-120	18.3	16.8	–	–
0-130	22.0	19.7	–	–
Standing ¼ mile	13.3	13.1	13.6	14.2
Max Speed (mph)	176	181	est 178	180.1

Autofolio

more efficient, it was decided, finally, that the latter solution was more practical. The reasons given were engine cooling, weight saving and ease of manufacture. The first sketches had been made in early 1978 but it was not until late 1981 that the ultimate shape was finalised and accepted. Pininfarina then made up a full-scale polystyrene model, which was further refined, before a further model was built in resin and used for wind tunnel testing. This one was subjected to the wool tuft treatment. In other words, short strands of wool were attached all over the body and their behaviour studied in the wind flow.

Initially the model was solid without any apertures and retained the sloping window over the rear deck. The next stage was to open up the side radiator apertures and study the flow around this area. The flow into the apertures was measured to ensure that it was sufficient to carry out the necessary cooling task without having to widen the body any further to enlarge the vents. It was also important to monitor the flow to ensure that the shape created a good flow into this region without causing undue turbulence or adversely affecting the airstream.

Apart from styling considerations, regulations decreed that the apertures must have some form of grille and so the slats were carefully designed to assist rather than hinder the ingress of air in this region. As the forward part of these vents was situated just behind the leading edge of the doors, the arrangement

and construction became quite complex.

Further work was done in the wind tunnel to locate high- and low-pressure points for the influx of cool air and extraction of heat from the engine bay and cockpit. Such cooling is particularly important but if these vents are incorrectly placed they can create adverse aerodynamic effects and impair the efficiency of the shape, which is all important in achieving the very high speeds. To ensure stability at these speeds, a good deal of effort was expended on shaping the rear of the body to achieve negative lift.

Whilst discussing styling it might be interesting to look for a moment at the creation of the interior. Indeed, Pininfarina stated at the launch that he considered the interior to be as important as the exterior and that each 'cannot be conceived separately'.

Two other, rather more radical, interior schemes were suggested to Ferrari by the stylists before arriving at the eventual concept. The first was a very 'clean' style with a red (what else) waistband carried from the middle of the doors round and below the dash in a continuous horizontal band. Above this was a padded roll which continued, on the passenger side, to run in front of that occupant before terminating in a rectangular console housing the instruments each side of the steering wheel.

The second scheme was even more adventurous. It had the appearance of being constructed out of large diameter tubes. These 'tubes' ran up each door casing to meet a horizontal 'tube' that travelled across the dash and from which sprouted a square box housing the instruments in front of the driver. The 'construction' was completed by another 'tube' which ran between the seats, horizontally, to the gear stick and then climbed to meet the dash 'tube'. It was all reminiscent of scaffolding and, to me, it looked more Germanic than Italian. Whatever, it was rejected.

Number three was much more conservative, as such designs go, and was, with minor revisions, adopted. The aim was to achieve a functional simplicity and to this end the radio lives behind a folded cover which harmonises with the rest of the fascia. There are no novelties for the sake of it and a note of practicality was sounded by the provision of a generous glove compartment in front of the passenger.

Ferrari's need to broaden its customer base meant that the BB replacement had to combine a new level of sophistication, the usual expectation of superlative styling flair and, of course, staggering performance. It was some challenge to meet.

Whilst Pininfarina were carrying out the styling work, the engineers at Ferrari were busy further developing the flat-12 Boxer engine. Having taken the decision to re-enter the American market it was necessary to carry out some redesign work to ensure compliance with the ever-stricter emission regulations. If

introduction of fuel injection. Thus some improvement was urgently needed to maintain performance and quattrovalvole, as the Italians term it, was the obvious answer.

It was therefore entirely logical to apply the same solution to the flat-12's quest for more power. A four

the Ferrari flagship was going to compete with its rivals, more power would also be needed and some attention needed to be applied to improving torque for this was an area in which the Boxer had been less than brilliant.

Turbocharging might have been the answer but it was too radical a step for the Ferrari flagship, though they did apply forced induction to the 208 model in 1983. Four-valves-per-cylinder technology was becoming fashionable, however, and Ferrari had already been developing such a configuration for their V8-engined 308 models. These had suffered a power drop from 255 bhp to 214 bhp, for European models, and 205 bhp on those destined for the States, with the

valves-per-cylinder arrangement allowed exhaust and inlet valve overlap to be reduced which was very necessary because fuel injection is inclined to squirt a certain amount of neat petrol out through the exhaust when both valves remained open. This was obviously detrimental to the aim of keeping pollution to a minimum. Matters were also assisted by discarding the mechanical K-Jetronic fuel injection in favour of the more sophisticated electronic KE-Jetronic set-up also manufactured by Bosch.

The adoption of four valves per cylinder dictated some redesigning of the engine and a considerable amount of development on the testbed. By trying many combinations of inlet and exhaust manifolding, the

The depth of the side-strakes can best be seen from this angle. Ironically, this most eye-catching of features stems, in a sense, from the most mundane of requirements, that of moving the radiators to make room for the luggage!

desired characteristics of maximum power, but good torque, were finally achieved.

Having developed the engine on the testbeds, it was time to evaluate the unit in a prototype. Over a couple of years, six disguised prototypes clocked up a considerable mileage around the mountains and autostradas surrounding Maranello. The very first tests had actually been conducted on a rolling road, followed by running at Ferrari's private test track at Fiorano.

As the package was not a radically new concept, most effort was expended upon improving, and above all refining, the standards set by the Boxer. With the aim of making a very civilised Ferrari supercar, attention was paid to ride, noise, ease of driving, and practicality. One senses the Fiat influence exerting itself behind the scenes, or perhaps it was merely that more and more ex-Fiat men moved over to Ferrari and occupied positions of influence. Having come from a mass production background, it is hardly surprising that they should view things a little differently from their pure Ferrari colleagues, who might be more inspired, but probably rather less practical.

In an era when even the most modest small cars are imbued with excellent cornering capabilities, good braking and comparatively spritely performance, the pressure grows upon the manaufacturers of exotica to raise their standards in all departments to match the mundane in refinement and clearly exceed them in all-round performance. For the smaller companies, this no doubt presents some difficulties, and the presence of Fiat, albeit in a background role, can only have assisted Ferrari in meeting the ever more stringent challenges imparted by improving industry standards and creativity-stifling regulations.

Somehow one does not think of a car such as a Ferrari as having air conditioning, even in the eighties, but the American market demands it, and thus it shall be supplied. On the other hand a heavy clutch used to be part of the chararacter of a sporting car, or something to be lived with, depending on how you looked at it. During development, effort was put into producing a lighter pedal for the Testarossa. Likewise, uncomfortable cockpit heat and poor ventilation used to be the price one paid for electrifying performance once the road cleared. Not any more, as the development engineers addressed the situation. Effort was even put into making the exhaust quieter – on a Ferrari! Much of the time was devoted to fine-tuning. The distinctive radiator apertures had to be enlarged to improve engine cooling. A plethora of shock absorber and spring rates were evaluated to ascertain the best compromise of ultimate roadholding and boulevard ride. The high speed attributes of the unique Nardo test track in Southern Italy was particularly useful for the Testarossa. There are few, if any other, test tracks where it is possible to maintain this car's maximum.

The radiator intakes had, for safety reasons, to be covered in some way and thus the stylists came up with the novel idea of a grille made up of a series of horizontal slats.

As we have said, the Testarossa is an evolutionary Ferrari rather than a revolutionary one and thus the concept shares much in common with its predecessor, the Berlinetta Boxer. However, and not too surprisingly, the Testarossa's great quality is in the refining, or honing, of that concept.

With regard to construction, a tubular frame chassis was retained. Considering the small numbers in which Ferraris are made, it is just not feasible, even if so desired, to adopt a full monocoque construction. On the Testarossa, the chassis is described by Ferrari as 'of the sideframe type with steel trellis tubes'. Akin to the Boxer the Testarossa has a separate sub-frame which cradles the engine. This can be detached from the main square and rectangular tube frame for work of a major nature to be carried out. The sideframe,

which runs through the sill area, has sheet steel welded to it to increase strength.

For similar reasons the roof is steel, as are the doors, to assist with passing the essential crash tests. These steel panels are manufactured by the ZincroX process which is said to offer a complete guarantee against corrosion. The rest of the bodywork is made of aluminium.

Beginning at the front of the car and moving rearwards, a grille has been retained in the nose area though the radiator is, of course, no longer located here. The grille, of three black horizontal slats and seven vertical ones, is mainly retained for aesthetic reasons though air is ducted to the front brakes. Beneath this rather blunt nose is a chin spoiler that does not protrude beyond the plan view and is

finished in black, presumably to try and disguise this ugly, but necessary and fashionable, appendage. To the left-hand side (when seated) of this air dam is situated a duct which provides air to the air conditioning condenser. The blunt nose wraps around in similar flat fashion to meet the front wheels and the mandatory side flasher is situated here just in front of the wheel-arches.

This frontal treatment is far less stylish than the Boxer's but reflects the aerodynamic influences which played such a part in the Testarossa's styling and the search for ever higher maximum speeds, and stability at those speeds.

With the exception of the twin headlamps situated out of sight in the usual manner, the more graceful and gently curvaceous 'bonnet' panel can be raised, being hinged at the front. This panel has a further duct in front of the screen and finishes in a lip which stands well proud of the screen to keep the passage of air away from the wipers. With the bonnet lifted, the

main carpeted luggage area is revealed; this consists of a deepish, square central section, in which the space-saver spare wheel and 115/85 R18 tyre sit, and shallower square areas atop the wheel arches. The available storage space amounts to some 3.5 cu ft.

Not surprisingly the windscreen is flush fitting and bonded to the steel pillars and roof section. The screen is raked very considerably, and affixed to the side pillars are the controversial wing mirrors, or 'organic growths' as someone described them! Initially just one of these was fitted, to the driver's side, but later a second growth appeared.

The doors carry the beginnings of, and indeed the greater part of, the even more controversial side vents for the radiators. The five side slats begin about six

inches back from the leading edge of each door and become deeper as the door panel proper flows inwards. The slats are pressed in steel and bolted to the door skins. An angled, vertical, black panel, which commences at the rear door edge and continues rearward in the adjacent wing area, assists in ducting the air on its intended route to the water radiators and oil cooler.

The doors have visible, key-operated locks situated near the rear of the door and a handle located out of sight, above the top slat. The gently curved side windows are surrounded by frames and are raised and lowered electrically, with the exception of a small, framed triangular quarter-light at the foremost point.

Rear three-quarter visibility is aided by one further, fixed, side window on each side, again surrounded by a black frame. Behind the left-hand window, the single fuel filler flap is situated in the flying buttress. Curiously this is opened by a key inserted into the visible lock rather than by the neater arrangement of having a release control located internally. Pininfarina badges are located behind the conclusion of the idiosyncratic side vents and ahead of the rear wheels.

The rear window is vertical and its ends curve to blend in with the inner line of the flying buttresses which are not too prominent and peter out a few inches from the tail. The buttresses have a narrow, flat, top section which is used as an air outlet and gives the effect of a black stripe. The horizontal plane of the engine cover is all-black and covered in slats, akin to the front and rear grilles, with the exception of the centre area which is surmounted by a square, bevel-edged red panel keeping the elements from that which is the heart of any Ferrari.

The rear has no plan shape because the wings continue in a flat plane down the sides giving a rather heavy, slab-sided appearance. The ends are radiused and the tail concludes in a small spoiler lip. The engine cover and buttresses are hinged above the rear window to allow access to the engine compartment. The rear lights, uniquely non-circular for Ferrari, actually sit behind the five horizontal slats which make up the rear grille. Apparently this is a Pininfarina patent which is designed to keep the lights clean and has been licenced to other manufacturers.

The wedge styling is really nothing new and was a theme which probably started with Bertone's Carabo. Created by Giugiaro, when he was with that styling house, he employed it on his design for the Lotus Esprit and it is rather ironic that the latest version of

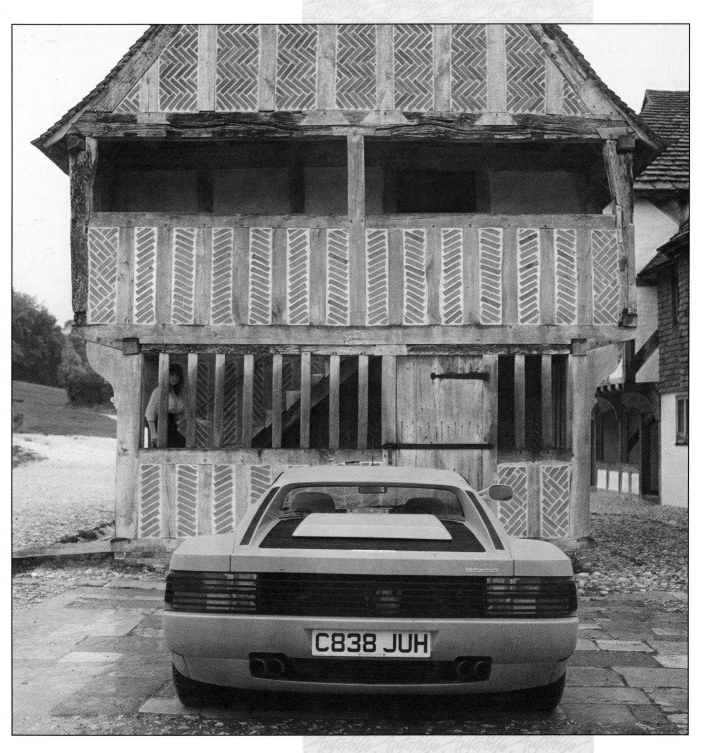

C838 JUH

that car has had the sharp edges softened in a manner reminiscent of the Testarossa. It is also rather ironic that the wedge-inspired Dino 308GT4 was compared unfavourably in the seventies with its more curvaceous sister, the 246GT. Such are the quirks of fashion and evolution.

Suspension on the Testarossa is independent front and rear. At the front, double wishbones fabricated from tubular steel are employed, with anti-dive characteristics built in. Cast alloy uprights are used and the lower wishbones are wide-based and cross-braced. A combined spring and damper unit is positioned between each pair of wishbones, which are mounted

The Testarossa is generously equipped in the braking department with ventilated 12 in discs and four-pot calipers all round. The handbrake employs two small drums within the rear discs and servo assistance is provided by a Benditalia brake booster. If excessively heavy braking effort is applied, a relief valve operates with a view to preventing locking up of the rear wheels.

In spite of the relatively wide front tyres, the rack and pinion steering is not power-assisted; the weight distribution is 41/59 front/rear, so there is comparatively little weight on the front. The turning circle is a little over 39 ft and the steering takes three and a half turns

in rubber bushes. An anti-roll bar is fitted and is attached to the lower wishbone on each side.

The rear suspension follows the same lines but uses a pair of coil spring damper units per side, mounted adjacent to the wishbones which are, again, cross-braced. All dampers are supplied by Koni. The anti-roll bar is again mounted to the rearmost leg of the lower wishbones.

lock-to-lock.

The Testarossa sits on 16 in diameter wheels all round but, like the larger-engined Boxers, they are of different widths front and rear. The fronts are 8J and the rears 10J. To these are fitted, respectively, either 225/50 or 255/50 VR 16 Goodyears and 240/45 or 280/45 VR 415 TRX Michelins.

Turning now to the magnificent flat-12 engine, the

cylinder block and cylinder heads are produced in silumin, a lightweight aluminium and silicon alloy, by Ferrari in their own foundry. The aluminium cylinder liners (rather than the cast iron ones of the Boxer) are coated with Nickasil to reduce bore wear. Inlet valves are made of steel, while the exhaust valves are made of Nimonic steel. The twelve pistons are manufactured not by Ferrari but by Mahle. The crankshaft, however, is machined at Maranello from a solid billet of hardened and tempered steel, the bearing surfaces being nitrided.

The engine, strictly speaking, is not a true 'boxer' configuration, the definition of such an engine providing that the opposite pistons move in and out simultaneously rather than sequentially. In a true boxer engine each piston has a separate crankshaft pin. Though this configuration provides perfect primary balance, other less welcome stresses are not controlled as well and so the Ferrari designers decided when penning the engine for the BB that they would stick to their usual V12 practice of having two pistons to a common crankpin.

Where the redesigned Testarossa engine differs from the earlier production version is, of course, in having double the number of valves. The two inlet valves per cylinder are inclined at an angle of 20 degrees and the two exhaust valves at an angle of 21 degrees. The seats are cast iron and the guides made of bronze. Like the earlier flat-12, the Testarossa engine has twin overhead cams per bank but, for the first time on the production horizontally opposed 12, 'the valve timing control,' states a Ferrari press release, 'is obtained through special cogged tooth belts of the Goodyear Supertorque PD type which absorbs the thermal expansion of the engine, while avoiding abnormal stress on the belts themselves. The adjustment is made through a semi-automatic tensioner. The redesigning of the engine has produced a reduction in weight of more than 20 kilos compared with the previous two valve version and has made normal maintenance easier.

'The exhaust system is particularly efficient, bearing in mind the regulations in force. It has two main silencers and two smaller ones made in stainless steel.'

'The ignition system – the Microplex type – has been improved and allows optimum spark advance throughout the engine range.' The Magneti Marelli Microplex MED 120B electronic system, to give this box of tricks its full name, reacts to messages from sensors gathering information on throttle loading, engine revs

Elton John was given a red Testarossa as a 40th birthday present by his manager in March 1987.

Maradona, the soccer superstar, owns a black Testarossa. Michelle Burley, 25 year old Managing Director of the Mallory Park estate and European Correspondent of *Feathered World*, has a yellow Testarossa with the registration number CEX 1.

A white Testarossa is one of the stars of the TV series Miami Vice. Originally the production company used Ferrari replicas built specially for the series – some court cases later they were using the real thing!

Autofolio

and intake manifold vacuum. There is a socket for a diagnostic device to be connected up for tracing problems, and dual coils and dual distributors are also part of the impressive specification.

'Spark plugs, with a stem thread of 12 mm diameter, have also been used on the Testarossa, as they have been for the GTO model, in order to obtain the best position in the combustion chamber.

'Lubrication is provided by a system of two scavenge pumps and one pressure pump, an oil reservoir and a thermostatically controlled radiator.'

The Bosch KE-Jetronic fuel injection has been retained. It was originally fitted to assist in passing the Federal emission control regulations and obviously with the Testarossa targeted at the US market such considerations remained uppermost in the engineers' minds.

As with the Boxer, the Testarossa engine is mounted north-south with the transmission below. The drive passes from the crank to the Borg & Beck $9\frac{1}{2}$ in ($8\frac{1}{2}$ in on Boxer) clutch and thence to the gearbox through a train of three helical gears, the last driving the mainshaft. The five forward gears all have the benefit of synchromesh as you would expect. The ZF limited-slip differential has the same final drive ratio as the BB, namely, 3.21:1, with 45 teeth on the crown and 14 on the pinion.

The interior breaks rather with Ferrari sports car tradition being rather more luxurious. Its design reflects the company's aim of producing an increasingly sophisticated, softer car to appeal more to the Americans.

Being such a large car, it is not surprising that the cockpit is generously proportioned even though that is not always the case with mid-engined cars. It is now an oft-quoted comment, but Squazzini, the Managing Director at the time of the Paris launch, referred to the car as 'a 300 kilometre per hour living room'. This has been Anglicized to become quoted as 'the 180 mph living room'.

Ferrari are keen that the Testarossa should be considered a practical long distance touring car. An important factor in this, apart from performance and reliability, is obviously driver and passenger comfort. Considerable effort has gone into producing excellent seats and they are electrically adjustable for rake, height and position relative to the controls. The seats, in smooth leather, are trimmed in hides supplied by Connolly Brothers.

The instrument binnacle houses the speedometer, tachometer, oil pressure and water temperature gauges, and a variety of warning lights including ones to indicate the fact that the bonnet or the engine cover has been left ajar. The fuel and engine oil temperature gauges live in the forward section of the centre console. Moving rearwards one finds controls for the heating and ventilation, electric windows and door mirrors, and suchlike. Amongst these sprouts the gearlever with its traditional gate.

Raising one's eyes, not to Heaven, but to the roof, one finds controls for the fog lamps, heated rear window, map light and interior light.

Apart from the luggage storage area in the nose mentioned earlier, there is space for such necessities behind the seats. To maximise effective use of this area of about 2.8 cu ft, a local Modenese firm of craftsmen in leather, manufacture tailored and suitably embossed items of luggage for the Testarossa. Three of these live behind the seats and a further three reside in the nose.

Nobody will be surprised to hear that red is the most popular colour specified by customers. Indeed it is a fact that there are more red Ferraris in existence today than ever left the factory as many people have repainted their older Ferraris in that almost statutory colour. However, the Testarossa can look equally dramatic in other colours including white and dark blue to name but two viewed by the author.

Whatever the colour, the Testarossa has presence, due, no doubt, to its dramatic styling, low line and, perhaps above all, due to its sheer size which guarantees an impact. Love it or loathe it, you cannot miss it!

PRESS REACTION

We have all read the glowing reports of Ferraris new and old as normally level-headed, even hard-headed, motoring journalists seem to drop all pretence of being objective and rational as they eulogize and so nourish the continuing Ferrari aura. In this way the legend is self-perpetuating, but is it really deserved? Is there really something that special to distinguish a Ferrari from some other fine motor cars on the market?

The aura is indefinable but, equally, undeniable. With the launch of the Testarossa, the tradition was continued as the top magazines were, as usual, effusive in their praise and generous in their assessment of the new Ferrari supercar.

In June 1985 Dennis Simanaitis and Wm. A. Motta of *Road & Track* reported on their trip to Maranello to test the first US specification Testarossa.

'A Testarossa, of any color whatsoever, is the reddest of red carnations. It's capable of marking your motorized progress among other drivers, leaving their lapels looking positively drab by contrast. Unless your order is in, however, you'll be joining the rest of us in less than sartorial splendour, for awhile at least. Even at a list price of $87,000, each US Testarossa is already spoken for, through the 1986 allotment. Ah, but we can dream, can't we?

'Our, and probably your, first look at this heir apparent to the fabled BB512 came at the 1984 Paris Salon. "The best news of all," we noted, "is that the Testa Rossa has been designed from the start with the US market in mind." Mark off our spelling of Testa Rossa to tradition and the story's late-breaking

exclusive nature.

'Later, Paul Frere visited Ferrari's Fiorano test track and shared his driving impressions in April 1985. "Surely the Testarossa deserves its glorious name," Paul concluded.

'In assessing the appearance of our properly red Redhead, Bill and I agreed that it's better looking in its aluminium and steel (the latter, only the doors and roof) flesh than in photos we had seen. But will its lines be as timelessly beautiful as the BB512's? As an avowed admirer of the BB, I'd say no; but others whose esthetics I respect will dispute the point. One thing I'll admit, however: The Testarossa's sidesaddle radiators are less obtrusive in actual viewing and, for some reason, their cheese grater grilles bother me less than those on the Mondial.

'The Testarossa looks aggressive – and wide. As indeed it is both, with its 4.9-liter flat-12 burbling out 380 bhp and fat Goodyear Eagle VR50 Gatorbacks bulging past flared fenders. The car's width is up there with the Lamborghini Countach's 78.7 in, at 77.8 in; the BB512 measuring 72.0 in, by contrast, and the Corvette coming in at 71.0 in.

'The Testarossa also goes through life looking a bit unbalanced, what with a mirror stalk growing organically from the A-pillar – but only on the driver's side. It seems that the A-pillar location precludes any hope of the driver seeing one mounted on the right, so none is fitted. Hardly the sort of solution one would expect of Pininfarina, I'd say. As with any mid-engined car, vision to the rear three-quarters needs all the reflected reinforcement it can get.

'In fact, though, I found the Testarossa far more habitable than its smaller 308 sibling. For one thing, the 308's head room forces me to rake the seat quite a bit more than I like. By contrast, the Testarossa's head room is a more adequate 36.0 in and, once rake and reach are set, everything falls readily to whatever appendages it's supposed to.

'. . . once used to the surroundings, I found the Testarossa's width not all that daunting.

'In our slalom, for instance, it worked its way up to a credible [sic] 63.5 mph, versus its smaller sibling's

60.9. While doing so, the car's steering offered excellent communication in both senses, as sender and receiver. Also, though not apparent from within, Bill tells me that the Testarossa's suspension looked fairly soft and I suspect this chassis lean provided yet another valuable input in probing the car's high cornering limits. It profited, by the way, from an educated and persistent throttle foot. Lift in a quick transition, and the Testarossa reminds you that there's considerable machinery riding behind you, exactly 60 per cent of the car's weight!

'There's a marvellous jet plane character to Testarossa's acceleration, continuing well beyond any limits of the Fiorano real estate. And Ferrari officials suggested that the local carabinieri might dislike my giving Bill opportunity to photograph confirmation of the car's calculated top speed on the autostrada. Seeing that it's 178 mph, I rather thought they would take this dim view on artful photography. Perhaps another time, and until then we'll just have to retain the term "estimated". Me, I think it's good for it.

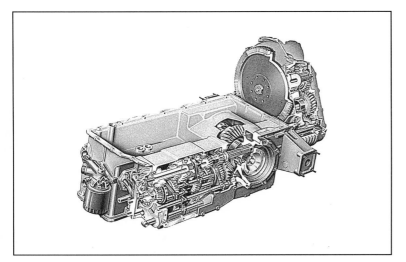

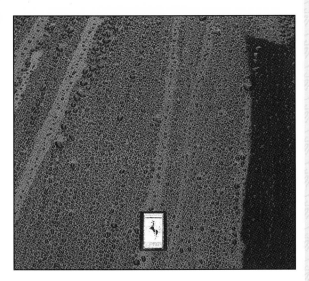

'The Testarossa's ride and handling reflect its development in northern Italy, a place where roads vary from quite good to downright nasty. The suspension communicates these changing surfaces very well; even a slight kickback in the steering – very much a Ferrari characteristic – carries useful information content. And this is combined with an absolutely astounding solidity of chassis and bodywork. I got the distinct impression that at least a couple of Targa Florios are built into this Ferrari.

'And while you're off running them, I guarantee you'll feel stylish as well. I remember photos from the Fifties showing Italian race drivers spiffed out nattily in coat and tie. The Testarossa is a car very much in this tradition.

'And don't forget the boutonniere, a bright red one.' The British magazine Motor wrote of the Testarossa in its issue of 13 July 1985.

'1984 will go down as a memorable year in the history of Ferrari. It is a long time indeed since Maranello unveiled two new cars both coveted by the wealthy and enthralling enthusiasts the world over. The magnificent pair of Prancing Horse machines couldn't have been more different in make-up or character.

'First the £75,000 homologation special, the GTO, of which only 200 will be built .... The other new Ferrari and the subject of this test is far from overshadowed by the GTO as it takes over from the now obsolete 512i Berlinetta Boxer as the flagship of the normal Maranello range. The £63,000 Testarossa is already the ultimate Ferrari for those unfortunates who may have missed out on a GTO.

'It is more than just a reskinned Boxer, being sleeker, lighter and more powerful than the car on which Maranello's senior supercar reputation rested for more than a decade. Even the name "Testarossa" – a powerful evocation of Ferrari's racing glory days when the V12 engined Testa Rossa of the late fifties and early sixties dominated sports car racing – is a confident assertion of superiority.

'Even had we not been constrained by the tightness of an engine that had barely covered 3000 miles and the wishes of an importer anxious for us to be gentle with its sole demonstrator, it is doubtful whether the Testarossa would have written itself into the acceleration league history books. In our hands, it sprinted from rest to 60 mph in 5.8 sec, hitting 100 mph in 12.7 sec and 120 mph in 18.5 sec; stunningly good figures and, perhaps, the best we could have hoped for given the dusty surface of an as yet unopened section of the M25, but not really in the Countach class (4.8, 11.3 and 17.4 sec for the pre-quattrovalvole 5-litre car).

'As impressive as its outright speed, however, is the Testarossa's flexibility. In fact, its fourth gear pulling power is little short of sensational ....

'It's one of the reasons the Testarossa feels so blisteringly rapid on the road; for its reserves of turbine-smooth power between 1000 and 7000 revs, there is no other engine made that can match it. Words like "peakiness" or "camminess" are redundant. The power just flows smoothly and strongly, the sensation of quickly gathering pace being massaged by a noise that is unique and almost indescribably exciting. It isn't loud by supercar standards, nor is it particularly complex. It's just a muted growl of extraordinary purity, unsullied by excessive transmission or cam chain whine (the belts are rubber) and the better for it.'

After mentioning that they had recorded a mere 12.1 mpg but suggesting that a more representative figure would be around 15 mpg, they continued.

'But soft-pedalling a Testarossa requires saintly restraint; the urge to exercise that magnificent engine needs constant watching and, in a straight line at least, succumbing to temptation is a fabulously rewarding experience, satisfaction coming as much from mastering the meaty slot gearchange as exploring the outer limits of the handling.

'For, make no mistake, this Ferrari doesn't have the race car responses or electro-magnetic grip of a

Countach. In second gear bends, the tail can be kicked out a few degrees under power as a matter of course; grip is good but not fail-safe. Even so, this is the more appealing side of the Testarossa's dynamic character. It's a fine machine for blasting out of medium-to-tight bends with your foot buried in the carpet; the resulting oversteer is flattering rather than intimidating.

'On faster sweeps, however, the big Ferrari inspires less confidence. Where you would expect it to settle into the corner and stick to its line with just a suggestion of stabilising understeer it feels edgy, almost fidgety. Bumps taken at high speed can upset the car's poise revealing a Grand Touring rather than overtly taut suspension set up. Neither characteristic particularly taxes the skilled driver's ability or, indeed, desire to corner quickly in the Testarossa, but they remove much of the pleasure.

' . . . Any owner will soon come to curse the thoroughly unconventional wing mirror. The view of the road it provides over the flowing line of the rear wheel arch is unrivalled but on entering a roundabout any approaching Cortina is completely masked from sight by the mirror.

'The joy of the Testarossa is a mighty and tireless engine which will go down in the history books as one of the finest ever to power a road car. It combines almost miraculous smoothness with a breathtaking spread of power but without temperament or uncouth rowdiness. The Testarossa also has tremendous presence on the road and real Grand Touring flair. It's less dynamically disciplined than Lamborghini's granite-muscled Countach but a vastly more refined machine that makes up in urbane practicality for what it lacks in purity of purpose. That much it shares with the Boxer; in other respects it's a mile ahead.

'At the end of the day it is a great Ferrari, if not the greatest. GTOs take some beating.' In September, 1985 it was the turn of the 'other' US magazine, namely Car and Driver, to test and report on the Ferrari flagship.

'When it comes to speed, 150 mph is the far side of the moon. If you want to explore it, you need a Chevrolet Corvette, a Lamborghini Countach, or a Porsche 928S. Or you can bypass the normal rocketry sources and plunge into the gray market, where a few current and past projectiles heed the call, answering with a howl; the BMW M1, the Aston Martin Vantage V-8, the Ferrari Boxer, and assorted Porsche Turbos. They belong in the fast lane. But they may as well park there for all the good it does them now. The new Ferrari Testarossa blows a hole through the middle and stampedes over the horizon so fast that these herds of high-dollar hot rods might just as well be cardboard cutouts.

'There is fast and there is faster than fast. The Testarossa is the latter. Top speed: 181 mph. Not a hypothetical or theoretical 181 mph, not a beer-claim speed, but a real rocking, socking, reproducible, you-want-it-you-got-it 181 mph.

'At 181 mph, the Testarossa is still in its element; a little busy and quite noisy, but squirming from cheek to cheek no more than a well-mannered nine-year old on an uncushioned pew. At sustained speeds of 140 to 160 mph, the car remains solidly planted. It wants a firm hand and a sure foot, but it tracks so well that you don't get caught out just trying to keep it in line. In hard cornering, understeer crops up reasonably early, reducing steering effectiveness, but much less so than in the Boxer. The Testarossa is also less likely to initiate unstable cyclings between the initial understeer and the lurking final oversteer. You can feel through the controls that such behaviour is in the car, and the feeling is strong enough to put off the faint of heart. The unassisted steering is heavy, slowish around town, and full of strong wriggle under firm braking over uneven surfaces, but it's spot on in the open territory where the Testarossa frees up and flies. Except for its slight cold bloodedness, the prodigious engine is perhaps the sweetest in our experience. Even nearing its 6800-rpm redline, it never feels as if any of those 48 valves in there were about to pop. Somehow you feel oil more than anything else, all so smooth and slick the whole thing seems to be made of oil itself, oil just thick enough to lubricate everything and just thin enough to keep everything whirring freely. It does whir freely: 0 to 60 mph in 5.0 seconds; 0 to 100 in 11.2

seconds; 0 to 130 in 19.7 seconds; the quarter-mile in 13.1 seconds at 107 mph. Not bad for a 3643-pound Italian girl with 181 mph of top end.'

The Australian viewpoint was given by Modern Motor in their March 1986 issue.

'I have never been a Boxer fanatic, as I felt it was somewhat gross and uninspiring on the track .... But as I have said before, I have yet to drive a road car that shows up really well in race conditions, unless it has been specially set up and modified for the track. The Boxer was a good looker and probably fun on an interstate journey (having sent your overnight bags ahead by 'plane) but I would prefer a front engined V12 412 automatic if I were ever to own a road going Ferrari.

'The Boxer is hardly your car for Sydney traffic and it is certain to arouse the interest of every patrol officer within the State whenever you nose it out onto the highway. So what did I think of the new Testarossa,

Autofolio

bearer of such a famous name, and the logical successor to the Boxer? The looks are very much a personal thing – we all have our own idea of what attracts us and fortunately for both car makers and women alike, our ideas vary enormously.

'I rather tend to the belief that small is more beautiful than big, and so I consider a Dino more beautiful than a Testarossa, just as I find an old 1.5 litre Brabham more beautiful than an F5000. But in some eyes the Testarossa is big and beautiful. It is certainly a head turner in any company.

'It is interesting that 0 to 100 km/h comes up in under six seconds and today you have several European touring cars running barely two seconds slower. And the standing 400 metre in 14.2 seconds, while shattering for a road car, is a second slower than the old 2.5 Cooper Climaxes managed 25 years ago! Something to do with power and weight ... and the Testarossa does have a curb weight of 1829 kg fully fuelled and laden.

'But the day of the spartan interior, the thinly disguised race cars, which made Ferrari the legend it is today are long gone and now we have everyday comfort found in the everyday Japanese car – air conditioning, electric windows, central locking, electrically adjustable mirror and so on, and all adding their power-eating weight.'

After discussing the values of older Ferraris and the ridiculous way they have appreciated, David McKay concluded as follows.

'The question now is: will the present day Testarossa ever appreciate to the same extent as the old timers? We'll know the answer in another 30 years .... Meanwhile, it has to be one very special toy to have in your garage and to hell with 30 years' time!'

In the October 1987 issue of Motor Sport, Alan Henry compared a venerable 275GTB/4 with the latest machine. He was ecstatic about the front-engined car and no less so about the mid-engined one, though a very different animal. Regarding the newer car, he had this to say.

' ... if it wasn't for the harsh ride, the bump steer and the low driving position, you could be relaxing in limousine luxury. Then you change down into second – and hope you are quick enough to grab third before the electronic rev-limiter cuts in ....

'Suddenly you have 390 bhp working hard for you in one direction, that 82x78 mm flat-12 hurling you towards the horizon amidst a glorious cacophony of sound. Not as melodious as the 275GTB/4, more a

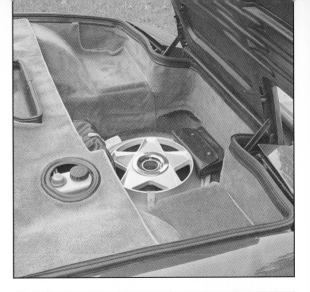

Space-saver spare wheel takes up a substantial portion of the limited luggage space.

harsh flat metallic bark, but every bit as attractive to the true Ferrari buff in its own way.

'The Testarossa is a spectacularly styled creation, with heavily louvred panels on its doors ducting cool air into the engine compartment. Devout Ferrari fans say that its lines are not so well balanced as the 512BBi (the beloved Berlinetta Boxer which it supplanted in the Ferrari range) but that is purely subjective opinion. I found it breathtakingly impressive, both to look at and to drive.'

PRODUCTION

Though retaining traditional elements, the whole Ferrari factory and most of the production processes have come in for considerable change in the eighties. In many ways the Testarossa is an inseparable part of that evolution.

In the fifties, Ferrari production averaged just 75 per annum, increasing from 26 to 248. In the Swinging Sixties output rose from 306 to 619, an average of a shade under 500, with a peak of 740 in 1965. The figure jumped to 928 in 1970, increased into four figures in the early part of that decade, fell back a little and then rose to a figure of 2221 by 1979. Production has continued to rise with the 3000 mark being exceeded in the mid-eighties and with a total of 3942 cars being built in 1987.

These increases in production have not been easy

because a Ferrari is, of course, traditionally a largely hand-made car. Most of the operations are labour intensive and many require highly skilled labour. Raising output, therefore, means employing more skilled labour, a scarce commodity in itself, especially in modern times.

Apart from the problem of finding and keeping suitably skilled workers, another aspect becomes a pressing consideration with increased volumes, namely, maintaining quality. We have seen many firms suffer from the malady of variable quality and the resultant customer dissatisfaction in recent times. With a company of Ferrari's reputation and one that is charging a considerable sum for its motor cars, quality must be maintained.

Although the Testarossa has a fair amount of overhang at the front, it is, in fact, not possible to see the bonnet from the driving position. Deploying the headlamps when manoeuvring in confined spaces is a useful ruse.

Autofolio

Furthermore, customers' aspirations have changed over the years. Perhaps this was inevitable with the larger market that Ferrari is trying to create and/or satisfy now. In the early days a Ferrari was bought by a diehard enthusiast who was prepared, perhaps even conditioned, to accept many shortcomings. The car's pre-eminent performance made up for the negative aspects, or perhaps the car, as with many, was bought for competition purposes.

That was fine when you were selling 75 cars a year, or even 500 worldwide, but it is a different matter when you are marketing 4000. Inevitably one's customer now is a different sort of chap. He has probably been brought up on mass production cars, and they have changed dramatically over the last couple of decades. He now expects even a Ferrari to be a civilised, reliable car.

Thus the Ferrari factory faced the major challenges of producing more cars, but also of maintaining, or perhaps improving would be the more appropriate word, their quality. Many experts have told me over the years, that a Ferrari consists of a marvellous engine – and that's it; the rest of the engineering, and the quality of construction, leaving a great deal to be desired. But then, the assertion goes, Ferraris have always been built to travel quickly, and little else.

I cannot help but be reminded of Sir Peter Ustinov's brilliant skit on sports car racing, the Grand Prix of Gibraltar, in which he impersonates many famous characters of fifties motor racing. The brakes

fail on one of the Fanfanis, and the driver calls at the pits to complain. Interviewed about the problem, Signor Fanfani says, 'It takes a genius to make a car go fast. What do you want to talk to me about brakes?'

Returning to the subject of production, apart from increasing output and improving quality, it was increasingly necessary for the factory to be flexible in its operations. This was dictated by the growing range of models, and also the increasing complexity of different specifications demanded by the bureaucracies of importing countries.

In order to trace the roots of recent developments, it is necessary to go back to the early-to-mid-sixties. At this time the Ford organisation decided that it wanted to go motor racing and, amongst other things, win Le Mans. One way to do this would be to purchase an existing and successful team. An approach was thus made to Ferrari and negotiations appeared to be close to finality when Ferrari broke off discussions and withdrew.

Due to the enormous prestige which Ferrari brought to Italy and in particular the Italian motor industry, Fiat had for some years been secretly making large contributions to the team's budget. Not surprisingly, Fiat were unhappy at the prospect of the Ferrari name being bought up by the Americans. Pressure may have been brought to bear behind the scenes by Fiat or maybe by the Italian government with whom Fiat had close ties. Whatever, the deal came to nothing and in 1965 the two Italian companies agreed to collaborate on the building of a V6 2-litre engine. This was to used in the Ferrari Formula Two cars, but impending regulations dictated that such engines must be based upon production units of which a minimum of 5000 per annum were built.

Quite obviously it was not feasible for Ferrari to build this quantity of cars but in conjunction with Fiat this became a practical proposition. Thus were born the Ferrari and Fiat Dinos.

In 1969 this relationship was taken a step further when Fiat acquired a 40 per cent holding in Ferrari. Of the remaining 60 per cent, Pininfarina owned 1 per cent, Piero Lardi-Ferrari owned 10 per cent and Enzo Ferrari retained 49 per cent of his company. Thus the 'marriage' was formalised. Ferrari would continue to run his beloved racing team, and Fiat would assume responsibility for the production aspect. Sad though it might seem that the old autocrat had lost his total control, it made admirable business sense and secured the long-term interests of the Ferrari company and name.

Wisely Fiat did not make changes overnight and it was not really until the eighties that major changes

began to be put in motion. Production, however, had been gradually increased and, for the reasons outlined above, it was necessary to improve productivity, quality and flexibility. The answer, it was decided, was the adoption of something known as a Flexible Manufacturing System – or automation and robotics, to explain the jargon.

At first sight the idea of robots in a company such as Ferrari seems an anathema. It is true that the final assembly is a labour-intensive operation and it is difficult to imagine the production of this car ever being fully automated. There are many machining operations, however, particularly in engine manufacture, that are repetitive and logical. These areas lent themselves ideally to automation where robots, able to perform a number of functions, could handle the skilled machining and achieve a consistency that no human could.

Ferrari is unusual amongst the smaller manufacturers in having its own foundry. Created at Modena in 1954 and moved to Maranello in 1958, the foundry has played an important role in the Ferrari story for it allowed the company to build the myriad

Autofolio

41

engine sizes and configurations that have been the basis of Ferrari success over the years. High standards are obviously required and it is felt that sub-contracting would not be the answer as the standards are too exacting for larger firms to achieve consistently and the quantities too large for the smaller specialists.

Aluminium and magnesium items are cast in the Ferrari foundry, magnesium being being used mainly for the racing cars and for certain parts for models such as the 288GTO. There are no facilities for casting steel and so crankshafts are bought in, though they are machined and balanced at Maranello. The Testarossa's engine, transmission and suspension castings are created in the foundry, however.

The process begins with the preparation of the moulds, or matrixes. These are coated, either with earth from Savona or sand from France, to facilitate removal of the cast item. For less complex items, a finished component is used to mould the sand to shape. By injecting carbonic gas and bonding agents, followed by baking, the matrix is hardened and then further heated with a blow torch to purge it of harmful gases and humidity. The final mould may be made up of a series of smaller moulds created in this way.

Meanwhile alloy ingots are being heated to 600°C in the underground furnaces. Some 500 kg of molten aluminium is then passed from the furnace into a crucible, where a small sample is extracted for

checking. This is chemically analysed in the laboratory adjacent to the foundry.

If all is well, the moulds are filled with the molten aluminium. Each Testarossa block takes 50 kg of the liquid alloy and thus 10 blocks are cast at a time. After hardening, the item is heated for six minutes before being removed from the matrix by vibration. All the processes are controlled for temperature electronically. The excess 'flash' is knocked off with a hammer before the casting is trimmed with a band saw or more generally a circular saw. The casting is polished and then hardness tests are performed.

The cast item is then stamped with certain information such as the part number, drawing number, the prancing horse, date and, on blocks and cylinder heads, an employee identification code.

As a result of the partial automation of some of these processes a single person has replaced the three previously employed in this area, and as many as 70 flat-12 blocks can be produced in a day. The skilled forming of the matrixes is, however, still a labour-intensive job and it is difficult to see how this can be streamlined whilst traditional sand-casting techniques are retained.

Sample castings from batches are further checked in the adjoining laboratory. These tests include magnifying the structure 1500 times, X-raying the component and analysing with a portable spectrometer and a 1500 volt spectroscope.

The next stage is the machining of the castings and here the automation has made an enormous impact. Beginning with just two pilot machines in 1984, these were supplemented by seven more six months later, and five more in 1986. Together with a multi-function post, these machines, which are made

by Mandelli, form the basis for the Flexible Manufacturing System.

The casting to be machined is transported automatically to the appropriate machine, and various operations are carried out. These include drilling, grinding and tapping as the rough casting, which sits on a bed which can be revolved, is transformed into a finished item ready for building up. These Mandelli machines can carry out 30 tasks and are programmed to cease functioning when worn cutting tools need changing, or a tool breaks. The machines are controlled by a Digital VAX 11/750 computer which, it is said, can handle a million instructions a second.

Apart from machining to tolerances of 1/100 mm, the automation has also led to a reduction in capital tied up in stock and improved stock control. Somehow one does not think of Ferrari having to consider such mundane accountancy matters as do 'normal' companies.

Another down-to-earth problem that one does readily associate with a company such as Ferrari is union problems. Nevertheless the firm has had its fair share in the past but the workforce accepted the

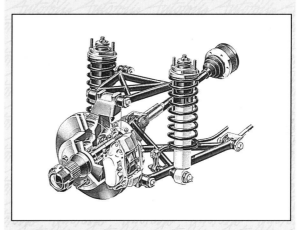

automation realising that the company could not survive without moving with the times. In fact, the workforce has increased in number in spite of the robots because production totals have been considerably increased. Realistic attitudes to automation, and training to use such modern wizardry, were both assisted by the nearby Istituto Professionale Statale per l'Industria e l'Artigianato A.Ferrari, or in plain English, the Ferrari college.

Engine assembly commences with a crankcase

which started life in the foundry. To this are fitted the main bearings, crankshaft and cylinder liners. These are followed by the twelve pistons, con rods and big end bearings, and to this assembly are mounted the built-up cylinder heads. Meanwhile the transmission units are being assembled and, following the fitting of the engine ancillaries, fuel injection and electrical systems another flat-12 is ready for testing. Each unit is run for a minimum of four hours and a variety of checks are made during this time. A tolerance of +/- 3 per cent compared to the ideal power curve is deemed to be acceptable.

So far the process of casting, machining, assembly and testing will have taken 140 hours.

Meanwhile the chassis and body are being built 150 miles away at a small company by the name of ITCA. The steel roof section and doors are rolled by hand, as are the other panels in aluminium. In an effort to combat corrosion Ferrari have developed a process by which they coat the steel panels and which they term ZincroX. The steel is first coated with zinc, then chrome and finally chrome oxide.

A chassis of rectangular and square tubing may seem a little old-fashioned in this age of monocoques but Ferrari claim that a tubular frame is, in fact, more rigid than one of monocoque construction. Quite apart from that they argue that it is easier to produce the different variations that the Type Approval regulations in various markets decree, and whereas it would take a year to introduce a modification to a monocoque, it can be achieved in only a month with the more traditional chassis.

From ITCA the bodies and chassis are transported to Pininfarina's nearby factory at Grugliasco. Here the bodies are first degreased, rinsed and dipped in zinc phosphate. From a drying oven the body/chassis units are immersed in an electrically-charged primer, cured and given two further coats of primer. This is followed by the application of mastic sealer to all inner panel seams and then by undersealing.

The bodies are then rubbed down and given another coat of primer before receiving a coat of paint. This paint is also electrostatically charged and covers all the accessible areas of the shell. The remaining areas are sprayed by hand with the interior given a coat of matt black. The exterior is completed with a lacquer coat and final drying in an oven.

From here on the car goes down the trimming line and such items as glass, wiring, body trim, electrical parts, sound deadening, air conditioning, sealing rubbers, headlamp mechanisms, bumpers, steering column, heater, general interior trim and seats are fitted.

The trimmed body/chassis units are then ready to make their journey to Maranello. Here the braking and cooling systems are installed. The completed engine/transmission/suspension unit is then offered up on its own sub-frame to the main chassis from below. Moving onto a raised section the steering rack, front suspension, exhaust system, and finally the wheels, are fitted.

The completed car is then road tested before being returned for any mechanical rectification and for cosmetic inspection. With final touching up of any defects, the whole process has taken in the order of 500 hours.

BACK-TO-BACK

There are few things faster than Ferraris, other than perhaps their aura which precedes them. The aura is such that it is almost intimidating. Writers everywhere have perpetuated that aura by eulogizing almost every model for as long as anybody can remember.

We are now conditioned to expect something extraordinary, and automatically summon up every adjective in our vocabulary to pay due reverence to these automotive masterpieces from Italy. Like Bugattis, there is art in the blood as well as engineering, and the result produces an almost religious fervour amongst owners and devotees.

But is all this near-worship deserved? Was it ever deserved, and perhaps more to the point, is it deserved today? Is it heresy to try to separate myth and legend from reality and to attempt a rational assessment, or do the emotions establish a dominance over the mind upon actual acquaintance with this beast?

When I was asked to write this first book in a new series from Haynes, I was given a shortlist from which to choose a subject. I chose the Testarossa as by far the most exciting, though I knew it would be the most challenging. But what human, who happened to be a car enthusiast, would turn down the chance of better acquaintance with the Ferrari marque? So I was behaving irrationally already – a good start!

It may seem like a statement of insulting simplicity, but obviously to write about a car with any worthwhile knowledge and to assess that car, it is necessary to sample one. You would think that self-evident, and yet there are books that do not take this approach. We felt it essential to drive one and talk about the model from a position of some little experience, but furthermore we felt it would be of interest to assess the car in the light of comparison with one of its peers.

In a sense, this was the first problem. What should we choose? Interestingly, and I discussed this with a number of people, there was no obvious contender. The Lamborghini Countach is certainly the nearest, but it is obsolescent, for a replacement has been created in the form of the Diablo and, thus, one would have

The subjects of our back-to-back comparison, the Testarossa and the 365GTB/4, the latter being more generally known simply as the Daytona.

been comparing the Testarossa with a model which is half a generation apart, which would not be valid.

The 959 Porsche is too high-tech and comparison of that with an F40 would be more valid than with a Testarossa. On the other hand, the front-engined 928s and Aston Martins are a different animal being in this context a rather old-fashioned, or perhaps it would be kinder to say, traditional concept. It is interesting to reflect for a moment how many of the supercars, which by definition are supposed to be at the forefront of, if not technology, certainly progress and performance, have been around for a jolly long time. On further reflection, it is perhaps not so surprising from a business point of view when one considers the level of investment, the low volume of sales and hence the highly risky and long-winded return on capital.

Indeed few, if any, of these cars would be made if accountants ruled. Most are today a prestigious front for a large multi-national. We should be grateful to them for continuing to manufacture these splendid and eccentric anachronisms. They give their owners pleasure, and the rest of us something to dream of and write about, fuelling the legends.

So, if it was not to be a modern supercar, how about an older one? How about another Ferrari?

Indeed, how about the supercar of a decade ago? The Daytona might be described as the last great front-engined supercar, a view reflected in its staggering rise in value over the last few years, and particularly since the death of Il Commendattore. Such a trial, between the deposed King of yore and ostensibly the ruling monarch of today should make a gripping saga.

So that decided it – all we needed now were the cars!

Some three months later after numerous setbacks we had achieved our aim of tracking down and capturing two of these rare beasts. The difficulties encountered in doing this had done nothing if not help maintain the aura of exclusivity that shrouds the marque. It would hardly do though if it were easy to borrow either such car – like Bunbury, the mystique would be quite exploded.

Toward the end of the hunt, by this time downcast and frustrated about the promises made and then broken, I approached one of the main independent Ferrari specialists, who trade under the appropriate name of Modena. I felt it was really pretty cheeky just to phone up out the blue and ask to borrow one of their fast-moving (in more senses than one!) pieces of stock to put it through its paces. They could not have

It is difficult to believe that only 11 years spanned the passing of the front-engined Daytona and introduction of the mid-engined Testarossa, which was a refinement of the layout first tried by Ferrari in the little Dino and beautiful Boxer.

Autofolio

been more helpful. In fact, their stock was so fast-moving, that no Testarossa stayed around long enough for David Sparrow, our photographer, the weather and I to get our act together. Matters were resolved, however, when they suggested we contact one of their customers.

To our amazement, Paul Lennon not only said yes but then went on to be co-operative far beyond the call of duty.

Now we just had to find a Daytona, which would probably be an even harder task, especially considering the way their values have exploded in recent times. If my memory serves me well, in 1986 one could acquire one for rather less than £20,000. At the time of writing, £250,000 is nearer the mark. By the time you read this, that will probably seem cheap! The aura is thriving!

John Young was, some while ago, a victim of one of my articles on collections, and he has a Daytona. Tentatively, I telephoned him. I was aware that, unlike some, he is not neurotic about his cars and has his feet firmly on the ground. He is one of life's true gentlemen, and owns the oldest Mercedes-Benz dealership in the country (Rose and Young in Surrey), but most appropriately another of his garages, Cissbury Garage in Worthing, had recently become the official Ferrari dealer for Sussex. The Daytona was on show there, and, 'yes, of course you can borrow it,' was the generous answer to my tentative question!

John has a splendidly relaxed attitude to these matters, which I think is delightfully illustrated by one incident. When telephoning him to finalise a day for the test, he mentioned that he would not be available as he would be playing golf that day.

'Ah,' I said, 'would you rather be with the car?'

'No,' he said, 'I'd rather be playing golf!'

Paul Lennon lives in Woking and is a copper dealer on the London Metals Exchange. He had only acquired

the Testarossa a few weeks before the day that I met him to test drive it for the first time: 'I was lucky enough to be made redundant, and had another job to go to!' Paul is perhaps not the typical Ferrari owner, or should I say, what you expect the typical owner to be. Indeed, the car is almost bigger than his house, and getting the car out of his garage and drive was not an easy matter, consisting as it did of shuffling his company car and his wife's car.

'Is there room for my briefcase?' I asked half seriously. There was . . . by my feet on the floor!

Bearing in mind the intimidating width of the car, and in particular the fact that the rear is wider than the front, I was very happy that Paul should drive initially, through Guildford. The traffic was appalling – slow and erratic – but the car behaved impeccably: first myth shattered.

The car did not overheat. The engine was happy to tick over for ages, without any clearing of the plugs. The demisting appeared to be doing its job. It all seemed very sensible. Can this be a 'supercar'? Is this

48

the stuff of which legends are made? Outside Guildford, Paul pulled up. Now was the moment I had been waiting for, and dreading! It was someone else's car. It was his new pride and joy and it was very valuable. There was that width. There was all the performance waiting to be unleashed. And there were the stories I had been told about the difficulty of getting used to the car. It was a trifle daunting!

What I like about a car such as the Testarossa is that one puts it on rather then gets into it, though it must be said that this one was a rather baggy fit!

The interior feels large, at least in width, and contributes to the feeling of size. Nothing else does, because you cannot really see anything else. All that can be seen of the bonnet, if such is the correct description, is the trailing edge where it flips up to guide the air over the wipers. You know there are a few feet of motor car ahead of you, because you saw them before you climbed in!

The seat is reasonably 'laid back' but not ridiculously so. It is certainly extremely comfortable and whilst not hugging locates the body well. The pedals are slightly offset to the left, but not uncomfortably so. The steering wheel is relatively small, which I like for speedy reactions, and finger tip movement, rather than armfuls of lock.

The dash is not greatly to my liking – but that is a matter of style, of personal preference. The layout is fine, which is the important thing; the surprisingly large and nicely traditional speedo and tacho can be seen clearly, as can the smaller oil and water gauges. The fuel and engine oil temperature gauges are curiously placed at an appropriate angle to meet the driver's eyes, in the upper part of the centre console. Behind these, alongside the thighs, are a rather motley collection of assorted controls and switches. They look surprisingly plastic, illogical, and – one hesitates to say – cheap and nasty.

The dash is trimmed in leather, but this is not immediately obvious. I remember someone at Lotus once mentioning the difficulty of not making the stitching look too good as it would appear as if it had been done on a machine. Here the leather is leather, but it is so thin and lacking in texture that it is difficult to be certain. In comparison with, say, an Aston Martin, the interior is rather disappointing. The impression one gets is not of sitting in one of the world's most desirable motor cars. The effect is neither spartan nor luxurious – it is rather bland. But is the interior that important in a Ferrari?

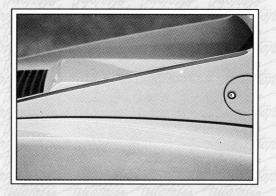

The price of a new Testarossa was quoted at £62,666 in mid-1985. A year later the Testarossa was priced at £78,950. By April, 1988 this had increased to £89,700 and delivery was two to three years. If you wanted instant delivery, a secondhand car would cost £120,000. By October of the same year, the factory price had further risen to £91,195. By 1990 the figure has reached £111,999. Secondhand prices appeared to have stabilised, or even to have dropped back a little.

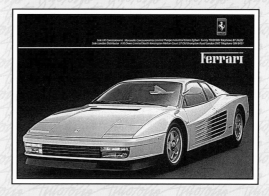

It is rare to see a Ferrari advert, but with overall production limited to just 4000 vehicles a year and a healthy waiting list, there is obviously little reason for Ferrari to advertise their wares.

Finally the moment had come to turn the key. I did so gingerly and the beast sprung to life behind my ears. It is a muted sound, very much there, but not uncomfortably conspicuous. The gear lever falls easily to hand and has the traditional Ferrari gate. First is selected by moving the stick left and back. It goes in easily, and with a few revs we move off.

I noticed that Paul had been avoiding second, which is advisable, it seems, even on the most modern Ferraris until the oil is well and truly hot. Initially the gearchange feels notchy and a little slow. The clutch might be termed heavy by some, but did not concern me. Above all, we moved away smoothly and without drama. Tootling gently along, I was immediately impressed by the torque. For example, the car pulled cleanly in fourth from 20 mph up a hill.

We were still meeting traffic but it was not necessary to keep going up and down the 'box the whole time. The engine seemed remarkably flexible and showed no dislike of stop/start, dawdling conditions.

The venerable Daytona was in production from 1968-1973 and was powered by a 4390 cc V12 engine which produced 352 bhp at 7500 rpm.

It was now raining lightly but the intermittent wipe dealt very adequately with water on the immense screen. This practicality was very impressive for such a car.

Vision seemed excellent or, to put it another way, did not seem to be a problem. I once owned a Lotus Esprit and so am not totally foreign to the slight constraints of driving a mid-engined car.

Rear vision is fine, though the quirky wing mirror took a little getting used to. Paul's car is one of the earlier ones and hence is fitted with just the higher single 'growth', and on the driver's side. He mentioned

that it could obstruct one's vision in certain circumstances. The first thing I noticed was that it seemed to be suspended in mid-air, it was so high and far away. It seemed so 'detached' that by the time my eyes had found it, it almost felt like watching a small television. It was better than nothing, but the field of view is limited. Electrical adjustment suddenly becomes less of a gimmick on a car like this. If nothing else the mirror certainly serves as a reminder of how the car bulges behind.

Paradoxically, that bulge did not seem a problem in practice. Rather like towing a trailer, if I may use so

base an analogy when talking of Ferraris, you drum into yourself that it is there and give obstructions a wider berth. Furthermore the front cannot be seen, so apart from the width of the cockpit there is no data on which to judge the width of the motor car anyway. For mundane motoring, I have a Granada Estate – my dog insists upon it – and so perhaps I am used to wider vehicles, but the Testarossa did not seem excessively, or embarrassingly, so.

So far the car was the lacking in intimidation, and almost sensible.

As the traffic began to clear, I ventured a little further with the excitement pedal. The response was instant and smooth. Fifth seemed perhaps a little lacking in outright umph from, say, 50 or 60, but then that is hardly fair criticism when one considers the prodigious top speeds of which this dramatic machine is capable.

The conditions were becoming increasingly frustrating. The drizzle had given way to a downpour. The traffic was heavy and desperately slow. The

The Daytona is actually 142 lb lighter than the Testarossa and, with a top speed of 174 mph, only around 6 mph slower when flat out.

Autofolio

overtaking opportunities, even in a Testarossa, were non-existent. This was all far from ideal, but again it confirmed what a practical machine the Ferrari engineers had developed.

Eventually, we turned off the A286 and took the B2178, to rendezvous as planned with David Sparrow. This road turned out to be well-surfaced, wide, quiet and made up of fair straights and fast sweeping bends. I could resist it no longer and, although the rain was now torrential, opened her up using near maximum revs through the gears. My passenger winced visibly.

This was more like it. The punch in the back was there, the handling felt reassuring, the brakes excellent,

and this was fun. For obvious reasons, I was taking no chances but using the gears we covered the next few miles very rapidly, and the atrocious conditions presented no problems.

Our venue for photography on this sortie – without the Daytona on this first occasion – was to be the Weald & Downland Open Air Museum. Here we found

a number of parties of school children being educated in what proper buildings should look like. The Ferrari acted like a magnet. Teachers lost authority, discipline was forgotten. Thank goodness we are still breeding car enthusiasts, though one wonders what sort of supercars they will dream about in 20 years' time.

Some weeks later arrangements had been made in conjunction with the weather men to bring the Testarossa and the Daytona together for a day of comparison testing and photography. This time Paul suggested that I should drive the Testarossa while he followed with a friend. Once again I was struck by how docile and well-behaved the car was in traffic. I did discover the flaw in the wing mirror design, namely, that going around an island, it obscured the road ahead to such a degree that one has to angle one's head to look under it.

Looking in the interior mirror, I was aware of the heat haze above the engine cover as the scenery moved around in an amusing fashion. In boyish manner I could not resist seeking out my reflection in the larger shop windows. But there was a problem in Guildford. The car was so low, that the railings at the edge of the pavement precluded any views. Eventually, a BMW garage obliged with large showroom windows!

As we motored through built-up areas, I tried to gauge the reaction of passers-by. Women did not seem to even notice it, but a number of men looked and turned as the car passed. And when we stopped for fuel, 'Ooh,' said the female cashier, 'is that one of those Testarossa things? My husband would do anything for a ride in one of those.'

An attribute which impressed me in traffic was the ability to increase speed in first smoothly without leaping forward. With the level of performance on tap, I would not have been surprised if it was all or nothing, but this was not the case.

Going through one town, a veteran car passed the other way. It towered over the Testarossa, which drew not even a glance from the intrepid driver. A few seconds later I had a heart-stopping moment as someone coming the other way left me little space in which to get through. God, I thought, I wonder how much wider it really is at the back.

Finally we left suburbia behind and I could briefly delve deeper into the Testarossa's character. Of one thing there is no question, the performance is prodigious. Winding it up through the gears is a most exciting experience. Third is a superbly long-legged gear and ideal for overtaking. There is tremendous punch available at any speed between, say, 40 and 70. You get the same sort of g-forces in fourth at 80/90. Apart from legal considerations, it was not practical on the single carriageway and twisty roads to explore anything like the maximum, but then ferocious acceleration is surely even more exciting than high speeds.

The roads dictated a number of squirt and brake sequences to maintain the exceedingly rapid progress, and this, apart from displaying the awesome acceleration, illustrated the excellent braking which more than coped with all demands. The large tyres ensured that we remained glued to the road, and the slight suspension roll did not seem excessive.

even islands taken at ridiculous speeds failed to unstick the generous rear tyres. One would have had to have been pretty brutal to get the rear to break away and that I was certainly not going to do merely to prove a point.

After a while I stopped to allow Paul to catch up. He was driving a saloon car of – by normal standards – ample pace, the performance of which he had been putting to good use, but it was interesting, I thought, how long it took him to arrive. I became convinced that he had taken another route, and had given up any thoughts of seeing him again before our destination when he suddenly hove into view. I mention

However, this style of motoring did highlight a trait that I did not enjoy. On braking hard from high speeds the front end gave a convincing impression of wilfulness, being decidedly skittish and weaving alarmingly. A less than smooth surface made this a bit too hairy for comfort.

Conversely the rear end behaved impeccably, and

this because I think it admirably illustrates how much time a really fast and competent car can save on a journey.

We successfully rendezvoused with David and I left them photographing the Testarossa whilst I went off to collect the Daytona.

Cissbury Garage is on the northern approach to

Worthing, and as I rolled up I could see the Daytona lurking at the front of the showroom, which is full of a small selection of John Young's fabulous collection. Andy Harwood, the General Manager, had started up the old girl the previous evening, and it quickly burst into life now.

Just climbing in one was aware that this a totally different piece of machinery. Indeed it was difficult to realise that there was barely ten years between them. It is no criticism but the Daytona seemed archaic in comparison.

The very first thing that struck me, as I climbed in, was the curious angle of the steering wheel. Rather than being presented in a vertical plane, it is quite steeply angled away from the driver, rather like, dare I say it, the wheel of a bus!

I took it very gently to start with to allow everything to warm up and out of respect for this venerable and magnificent piece of machinery. Also it gave me time to get better acquainted with her, and it took a little more time than the Testarossa. In particular the gearbox needed to be learnt.

The Daytona exuded more character, if only because it needed more getting used to, and was, if you like, more difficult to drive. Clearly there was none of the sophistication of the more modern car. There was less compromise, or versatility, depending on which

The Daytona was a good example of Ferrari's conservatism, sticking with the traditional engine position whilst its competitors had already begun to move the power unit to an amidships position.

way you looked at it. Also the Daytona felt very small after the Testarossa, which is curious because it is by no means a small car, but one does not feel so low.

I was on a dual carriageway and, with everything warmed up now, increased the speed very considerably. This was exciting living. When you are going fast in a Daytona, you know it! There is much more hustle and bustle about the car. There is a lot of wind noise, and the road surface is felt far more.

The V12 engine is less flexible than the flat-12. It will pull from 40 in fourth but is not happy in fifth. But this is a long-legged car, which goes on and on pulling up to unmentionable speeds. This performance is accompanied by the distinctive Ferrari V12 sounds. Whereas on the Testarossa the sounds have been insulated from the driver and though ever-present are not insistent, the V12 noises are all-pervading. One has the feeling all the time at lower speeds that the magnificent engine is just waiting for any half-excuse to be given free rein. It seems impatient.

In fact, the Daytona feels far more akin to a competition car. It is pretty basic. It is far from quiet. The ride is firm. The power is spread over a narrower band but, in the right gear, is constant.

Yet this is not to say that it showed itself to be impractical. It is not the sort of car you would want to drive regularly in heavy traffic – apart from being such

a waste – but it did not overheat or complain, though in fairness I did not encounter the same level of traffic that the Testarossa had dealt with so good-naturedly.

The steering, as John had mentioned to me, is ridiculously heavy when parking or manoeuvring at slow speeds, but once well on the move it is no problem.

The roadholding feels decidedly vintage after the 'glued to the road', massively tyred Testarossa and it is far easier to find the Daytona's limits. It is also possible to exceed them without risking everything. Through islands, for example, one can power the tail out without drama. That curious steering wheel angle does, however, inhibit fast cornering as it is not so easy to apply and unwind opposite lock in a hurry when the wheel points away from one.

The gearchange I found surprisingly sloppy with a lot of travel across the gate; certainly rather more than one might expect. The brakes seemed lifeless after the other car and required a lot more pressure but actually seemed very adequate. I remember Neil Corner once telling me that they do not like being used in quick succession to slow from 150 plus speeds. It was not a point I verified on this occasion! One does, however, need both hands on the wheel when braking from higher speeds at the approach to a corner where the surface is less than even. Nonetheless it is very stable at higher speeds.

Going through one town a Rover garage obliged with a window for the reflection. I have to admit to a twinge of excitement as I saw myself actually in a Daytona! This was something to tell them down at my local! It's that aura at work again.

Whilst stuck in traffic, a bunch of yobbos started walking towards the car. Wondering if they were going to turn nasty and take it out on the car, I thought, I know, I'll tell them it's a replica!

The interior is certainly a lot more sparse but not without character. It dates back to the days, perhaps, when Ferrari had yet to bother about such mundane matters. The pedals, ironically, are offset to the right, but again are not uncomfortable. It is not a car for having conversations in and although having the window down brought in the chill autumn day it was more than compensated for by the stirring exhaust note.

I have never known cars get out of the way so fast on a dual carriageway as they did when the Daytona approached. Stopping for petrol, one kind gentleman assured me that, 'that is a real car'. I had never been in any doubt.

Turning off the dual carriageway to make my way back to the rendezvous, the car felt even faster on the more claustrophobic roads lined with high hedges. It is certainly a more tiring car to drive quickly, but tremendous fun. The Testarossa is more relaxing due to

The amidships position of the radiators dictated that the body design would have bulging hips, which some feel is detrimental to driving. Nevertheless this innovative part of the Testarossa overcame a number of the problems associated with mid-engined cars, including that of running coolant pipes from front to rear.

Autofolio

the enormous reserves in all departments.

The Daytona certainly has more power than roadholding, whereas with the Testarossa these two characteristics seem more evenly matched.

The two cars are poles apart and it is very difficult to believe that there are so few years between them. They are not only very different designs, they are very different types of car. The Daytona is perhaps the last of the big, hairy, uncompromising Ferraris and thus has enormous character.

The Testarossa does not exude the same forceful persona being a more bland package, for the simple reason that it is aimed at a different market, or maybe the traditional customer has changed. One suspects that today's US executive does not have the patience to live with the vagaries of the older Ferraris, which were designed for tolerant enthusiasts and crude performance. The Fiat influence and the changing

market have combined to produce a tamed Ferrari that is perhaps the ultimate commuting machine. The Testarossa is most certainly a practical car.

I hope that last statement has not dented the aura!

Aside from the practicality, it cannot be denied that it is an immensely exciting car. The performance is highly impressive by any standards. For me it is a striking car rather than a beautiful one. I feel that the Boxer was the last beautiful Ferrari, and the Daytona leaves the Testarossa standing in this respect.

I am convinced that there are other cars on the market that are just as good as the Testarossa, but they do not have that unique name, and never will. The Testarossa is good *and* has the name. You cannot beat that because that combination of emotion and objectivity still equals 'aura'.

I tried to remain rational – but this redhead is heady stuff!

PRIVATE

NO FOOTPATH OR
BRIDLEWAY
NO UNAUTHORISED
OR FOREIGN-MADE
VEHICLES

C838 JUH

THE COMPETITION

Although the term was only coined in recent years, there have always been 'supercars', and a fair proportion of them have been manufactured at Maranello. In recent years the established Italian firm has had rather more competition with the birth of Lamborghini, De Tomaso and the 'upwardly mobile' Porsches. Although their compatriots, Maserati, have disappeared from the supercar scene, that august and typically British firm of Aston Martin soldiers on.

Inevitably each model has its strong points and its drawbacks. Some are more impractical than others. Every possible configuration and combination of engine and transmission position seems to be covered by the range that was available at the time the Testarossa joined this elite bunch in the mid-eighties. Though each is so different, you can be sure of one thing – each will have its own group of dedicated admirers, who will look at no other!

We will now take a look at the competition in the mid-eighties with a view to assessing how the Testarossa compared with its mighty rivals.

Lamborghini Countach QV
In many respects the nearest rival and the one to beat on top speed, if nothing else. An outrageous car with outrè styling that nevertheless has commanded, and continues to command, considerable respect amongst the most knowledgable and experienced of motoring writers. Given the four-valve treatment to maintain prestige and electrifying performance. Later updated again and then replaced, in 1990, by the Diablo.

Aston Martin Vantage
Utterly conventional and thus saddled with a rather old-fashioned image. However, a remarkably quick, well-balanced car that proves

that a well-sorted front-engined car can still compete admirably with the seemingly more exotic chassis configurations. Appearance was not been improved with sprouting of ugly front air dam. A very heavy but refined machine with good interior layout, excellent brakes and surprisingly good power steering. Probably the highest standards of workmanship, and truly still hand-crafted. A replacement introduced in 1989 and called the Virage relies on a similar concept but sports a new chassis and bodywork although it uses essentially the same engine.

The Daytona, in spite of being introduced some 16 years earlier, is quicker off the mark to both 60 mph and 100 mph than the Testarossa.

Performance	0-60	Max mph	Price	mpg	cc	bhp	Wt,kg
Testarossa	5.8	181	£62,666	19	4942	390	1641
Countach	4.8	183a	£65,900	14	5167	455	1422
Vantage	5.2	168b	£56,994	14	5340	368	1783
911 Turbo	5.3	160	£42,444	20	3299	300	1308
Pantera	5.5	139	£24,247	14b	5763	350	1407
928 S	6.5	149	£35,524	23	4664	310	1540
XJ-S HE	7.6	150	£23,995c	20b	5345	295	1755
Esprit Turbo	5.5	152	£23,440	25b	2174	210	1200

Prices given for March 1986

a–Countach S   b–estimated   c–1985 price, last year of manufacture

Porsche 911 Turbo
A car that seems to have been around for ever. With continual updating and improving of the original, basic package, the 911 has maintained its extraordinary popularity. With ever-increasing sizes of engine, performance has naturally improved and taken the car into the higher echelons. The Turbo model boosted it to the highest strata whilst wider wheel arches and wings gave the ancient shape the necessary image. Various writers have expressed reservations about ultimate roadholding and speed of breakaway as a result of seemingly archaic rear-engined layout. Good reliability and lengthy service intervals make this, perhaps, the most practical of the supercars.

De Tomaso Pantera GT5
This car lacks the image of the other supercars simply because it has neither a racing heritage nor an engine manufactured by De Tomaso. Indeed they use a very prosaic American V8 which, though lacking in upmanship image, gives the car considerable practicality and exhilarating performance. Packaged

for the States but not to be overlooked or underestimated. Curiously, though, like most of the other contenders, the car seems to have been around for an awfully long time.

Porsche 928S Series 2
Porsche surprised everyone when it 'went conventional' with the 928 and its smaller brethren. Seems curious that one company should produce two cars that seemingly compete with one another. However, the 928 is a different animal and though it disappointed a number of writers for its lack of supercar performance in its original form, the 'S' somewhat remedied that. A highly refined car that is bought by Rolls-Royce owners who want something more sporty.

Jaguar XJ-S HE
Incredibly ugly car that barely fits into the supercar mould perhaps due to familiarity. Well-engineered high speed express, with brilliant engine, but the accent is on refinement and comfort rather than sporting characteristics. Actually

went out of production for a while due to lack of demand and dreadful quality. Resurrected using more economical HE engine and widely vaunted improvements in quality. Disappointing car from a company with such a great past. Given an image boost with the introduction of the more stylish Convertible. Practical and comparatively good value for money.

Lotus Esprit Turbo
The Turbo Esprit would not be on everybody's list of genuine supercars, which is curious when you dispassionately consider its capabilities. It certainly lacks the image of the others, but perhaps it has been too cheap to get into their league. Certainly matters are not helped by Lotus's kit car heritage and former appalling reputation for quality and reliability. Superb driver's car that combines the late Colin Chapman's justifiably famous reputation for producing a car with brilliant roadholding and superb all round performance. Cheap but outstanding.

Anonymous

The owner interviewed here has owned a Testarossa and, indeed, has another on order in spite of his views, but wishes to remain anonymous rather than risk upsetting Maranello Concessionaires and his chance of obtaining future Ferraris!

'The Testarossa is a motorway car. It is too wide, particularly at the back. You can drive into the garage watching the front, as you would with a normal car, and of course the back's so much wider. If you are not careful, you crunch the back on the edge of the garage.

'Overtaking, particularly on country lanes, with cars coming the other way, twists your guts up so you don't enjoy driving it.

'The car performs well and handles well, and the ride is superb but to me it is not an adrenalin pump. It is too civilized – it isn't what Ferraris are about. I think the average Joe who buys a Ferrari does not do so for everyday use. This is only my opinion. If Ferrari, having done their market research, consider that people do want civilised Ferraris, then fine, do a civilised Ferrari. But they should do a parallel car that isn't civilised – a hairy beast, if you like. The last thing want to see on a Ferrari is four wheel drive. To me that would be a backward step. The only sort of technology that I think would be a benefit to Ferrari would be ABS braking. Apart from that, I reckon they should go backwards not forwards.'

I asked if he had had a Boxer, and if so how they compared.

'I've had about twelve Boxers. In performance, the Testa is obviously a better car. It handles better, rides better, and goes better, but it is not such fun to drive.

'I've ordered another Testa purely on the basis that I can't order a V12, because they haven't announced they're making one yet. So I hoping it will be long enough delayed for me to switch the order to the V12 – if they ever bring it out – because the suggestion is that they might bring it out in parallel, rather than instead of, and that the V12 will be less refined and more a driver's car.

'I am sure there are two types of Ferrari market in general terms. There is the real Ferrari enthusiast market, which does not want a civilised car and there's the ''poser's'' market which wants a civilised car – the South of France promenaders. I don't see why Ferrari can't cater for both.'

I asked if the car was a practical one apart from the width.

'Well, that's what makes it impractical, totally impractical. I live in the country and getting to the motorway really is nervewracking. In towns and cities, it's impossible.'

John Sager and Richard Downey

John is a New Zealander who at the time of our meeting was spending several months in Britain during which he had picked up his new Testarossa from Maranello Concessionaires, and was driving around this country before returning home later in the year. Richard Downey, by coincidence also from New Zealand, was doing exactly the same.

J.S. 'It's a love affair – no question about it.

'I have to confess that the first month or so with the car was a little daunting because of the width of the car, and the fact that the rear is wider than the front, and you've got that wedge shape working in both planes, in addition to which when sitting in the driver's seat, you cannot see any corner of the car completely. Although the visibility is absolutely excellent, the shape precludes your seeing the corners.

With the headlights up, you get a much better idea of the front of the car, but your rear quarters are lost areas to a rather incredible degree.'

R.D. 'You have got to use the side mirrors to reverse. If you don't use the side mirrors and just look out the rear window, you are going to clout the corners. It goes out about, what, fourteen inches further from the point that you can see. I've very nearly done it, it's so easy to do and you've just got to use those side mirrors.

'To start with, I was disappointed. I found the suspension was much softer than I was expecting and it didn't go round corners anything like I was expecting it to. In fact, I was with the Lamborghini people at the time and I honestly think that if they'd had one the right colour without the taxes paid, I would have done a deal there and then.

'But fortunately they didn't, because I found that the fact that I was so intimidated by the car was because I wasn't relaxed with it – I just wanted time with it. We had the shock absorbers hardened, which made a big difference, and now it's true love.'

With regard to Richard's initial disappointment, I asked him what he had owned immediately prior to the Testarossa and thus what he was comparing it with.

'I had a 1983 308GTS QV, which I'd had for a year, and I found it such a brilliant car. It was nimble and chuckable, and I expected the Testarossa to be the same. Another problem, too, because we were running it in, you weren't able to use the entire rev band and actually 'drive' the car. I would say of that initial 3000/4000 miles until I started really becoming used to the car, the main reason for the disappointment, was eight-tenths lack of driver ability, that was all. Now that I have driven the car I am a more competent driver behind the wheel.

'I found that the only complaint that I have, which is easily rectified, is that the exhaust is too quiet. It would be nice to have a bit more of a Ferrari sound to it.'

I turned to John and, mentioning that I had heard that they were too sophisticated, asked if he would agree.

J.S. 'I'm fortunate in that I've got a Daytona at home and that's got everything that is so totally and utterly Ferrari, whereas there is no question the Testarossa is more sophisticated. At the same time, it is a more usable car. You can really go great distances in it, in comfort, and arrive pretty fresh at the end of the

Like a number of great cars, the Testarossa is not of itself tremendously innovative but rather a refinement of a successful mid-engined concept. There is no doubt that the image of Ferrari has changed – to the extent even that one less than besotted observer was heard to describe the Testarossa as the 'top of the range Fiat'! Evidently he wasn't looking from this angle.

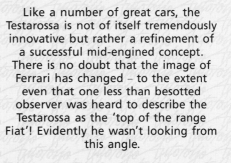

day and have enjoyed some very, very quick motoring at the same time.'

I quizzed John on whether he would prefer a modern Ferrari which was a little less sophisticated and, perhaps, soft.

'I don't think you can turn your nose up at improvements and development. I think that's wrong. You've got to continue development. But I, personally, do think it needs a stronger anti-roll bar.

R.D. 'The idea has been mentioned of having two Testarossas available, where you have a 'sports' Testarossa and a 'boulevard' Testarossa. Then those that are drivers can take the sports pack and those that want the car just for cruising down the boulevard, well, they can have the soft option.

'John hasn't mentioned it, but a problem has come to light on some cars; his is afflicted, luckily for me mine isn't. For some reason his Testarossa is over-servoed on the brakes. He can't do a nice double

The Testarossa interior is, perhaps, disappointing for a supercar, giving the impression of being very plastic and haphazardly designed. Certainly Ferrari interiors do not match the levels of opulence of, say, Aston Martin, which is curious when one considers the Italian names famous for leatherwork and design. The glove compartment and radio cover do, however, show flair in detail design.

declutch without jerking, not through his lack of ability, but simply because on touching the brake pedal, just with a featherlight touch, the car starts slowing down immediately. Leave it at the same pressure and ...'

J.S. '...it increases. With a constant pressure, you get an increase in braking, which I think is the discs warming up. They are such big discs and I think they need to warm up. They become more efficient with the increase in temperature so you get this feeling of increasing retardation with exactly the same pedal pressure.

'If you are heel-and-toeing, you tend to want to use the brake pedal as a fulcrum. On my Daytona the

pedal is just rock hard, and it is so beautiful to heel-and-toe on because you can lever against it and modulate your braking just with pressure and not movement. So I have to concur entirely with what Richard says, I would prefer a less servoed car.'

R.D. 'Talking to other people about that particular problem, apparently there were buyers who took them back because the wheels were locking up under braking at 30 or 40 mph in the wet. They have tried to correct it, but they don't seem to be able to. Why mine has not got it, I don't know.'

J.S. 'Of all the Testarossas I have driven, which is four, three of them are the same and Richard's is the only one that is not over-servoed; it's more pleasant to use because of it.

'I have found the car 100 per cent reliable at this stage of the game. I've done just over 6000 miles and I'm coming up to my second service. The build quality on this car is quite superior to my previous Ferraris, without doubt. This is the first Ferrari I've had that has had bolt-on wings, for instance. So they've changed quite dramatically their whole set-up. The fit of the panels is vastly improved. The paintwork is still not up to my standards of a paint job, but then I am probably being a little super-critical. I personally prefer a totally flat paint job, I don't want to see any orange peel at all in a handbuilt car, and these cars have orange peel in them – but so do Porsche and so do Mercedes. If you get the angles right, you can see it in the paint.'

I enquired of John whether he had owned a Boxer or had any experience of them.

'I have not owned a Boxer but I have used a 512 Boxer for 500 miles. The Testarossa is very, very similar and quite obviously a development of the Boxer. I definitely consider it is a superior car.'

R.D. 'We were doing 160 mph quite easily over in France a couple of days ago; and you put your foot down and it just keeps on going. I got up to 175 and it was still going. Then I chickened out but I felt the engine had more to go.'

I asked Richard how it felt at that speed.

'It doesn't sit on the road as well as I would like it to. It's still very good considering you're doing that speed. The road surface was a little bit bumpy and undulating. I have driven a Lamborghini Countach at the same speed and I found it far superior in aerodynamics and in feel on the road. When I put my foot on the brakes for a hard stop from 165 in the Lamborghini, I could have taken my hands off the wheel. It was just an incredible sensation. That's where

I think the suspension is just that little bit too soft on the Testarossa. As far as the aerodynamic Cd goes on the Testarossa, it is far superior, but I fell in love with the Countach straightaway. Admittedly that was just immediately after having taken delivery of a super-soft Testarossa.

'I think there is a place for both of them. They are like chalk and cheese. The Testarossa is far superior in some areas and the Lamborghini is superior in others – mainly from a driver's point of view. When you are driving at eight- or nine-tenths – it is a funny feeling – it just inspires so much confidence. The Testarossa, whilst it was really good, and far superior to your average car, just didn't quite have that edge.

'But probably if you looked at it from an overall point of view, for the average person, unless they liked being a real animal behind the wheel, the Testarossa would be the more suitable car. But I like being an animal!'

J.S. 'Richard is a harder driver than I am, I have to admit! We are coming up to similar mileages and I've

The shape of things to come. In November, 1989 Autocar & Motor published this impression of the 1992 Testarossa, which they stated would have 400 bhp on tap thanks to newly developed heads. By the time of going to press it was clear that 420 bhp would be available to achieve a target top speed of 186 mph and a 0-60 mph time of less than 5 seconds.

got more tread left, and I think that's the proof!

'I took my car to the Modena test day at Castle Combe circuit. In the morning it was raining very heavily and most people were not out on the track. But I wanted to get out there so I thought I had better find somebody to show me the way. I came across an older racing driver by the name of Terry Sanger, who

better. In fact, the whole ride has actually improved by hardening the shocks!

'You have to remember that they are building for the American market now. It also makes for a more usable car in more situations and conditions. My wife loves and enjoys it. It is the easiest Ferrari I know to drive. The clutch is beautiful to use and the lightest I

was apparently a touring car champion in the past. He is a very, very smooth driver and we went sailing round Castle Combe. I came in absolutely enthralled with the run because I realised just what you could get the car to do. It really was there to be got.

'It is a driver's car. I have subsequently had my shock absorbers hardened up and I find the car much

have ever driven on a Ferrari. The controls are very similar so there is a nice harmony between all the controls. The gearbox is still very Ferrari, though!

'The public response to the car is the best I have ever had in any Ferrari I've owned. More people recognise it and know what it is than any other Ferrari.'

Manufacturer Ferrari Esercizio Fabbiche Automobilie Corse SpA

Engine

Configuration	Horizontally opposed cylinders
No of cylinders	12
Bore and stroke	82.0x78.0mm (3.23x3.07in)
Capacity	4942cc (302 cu in)
Valve gear	Dohc per bank, belt driven, 4 valves per cylinder
Compression ratio	Variously given as 8.7:1, 9.2:1 and 9.3:1

Max power	390 bhp (287 kW) at 6300 rpm (DIN)
Bhp/litre	78.9 hp/litre
Max torque	361.6 lb ft 490 Nm at 4500 rpm (DIN)
Red line	6800 rpm
Block	Aluminium alloy
Cylinder head	Aluminium alloy
Ignition	Marelli Microplex MED 120B electronic
Fuel injection	Bosch KE-Jetronic, per bank
Fuel requirement (US)	Unleaded 87 octane

Bearings	7 main
Cooling	Water
Lubrication system	Dry sump with oil cooler
Oil capacity	27 pints (15.5 litres)
Emission control equipment, US	3-way catalyst, oxygen sensor, air injection for cold start

Transmission Type 5-speed all-synchromesh manual gearbox
Position Rear mounted under engine
Manufacturer Ferrari

Gears
Gearbox ratios
1st	3.319
2nd	2.014
3rd	1.526
4th	1.167
5th	0.875
Reverse	2.532

Final drive ZF limited slip differential, hypoid bevel gears
Final drive ratio 3.21:1 (14/45)
Transfer gear ratio 0.93:1
Clutch Borg & Beck 9½ in double plate

Body and chassis
Chassis construction Steel tubular
Body materials Steel roof section and doors, otherwise aluminium panels, fibreglass reinforced bumper panels
Designed by Pininfarina
Built by ITCA

Steering
Type Rack and pinion
Assistance None
Turning circle 40 ft (12.2 m)
Turns per lock 3.45

Brakes
Type Hydraulic, servo-assisted
Circuit Twin independent, split front/rear assisted
Front 12.16 in (30.9 cm) ventilated discs
Rear 12.20 in (31.0 cm) with 4-pot calipers
Handbrake By cable operation to integral miniature rear drums

Suspension
Independent by double, wide-based wishbones, Koni dampers, coil springs and anti-roll bar.

Wheels
Front Speedline five spoke cast alloy, 8Jx16 in
Rear Speedline five-spoke cast alloy, 10Jx 16in
Spare Spacesaver 3.25 in (8.25 cm) alloy rim

Tyres
Front Goodyear 225/50 VR16 or Michelin 240/45 VR 415 TRX
Rear Goodyear 255/50 VR 16 or Michelin 280/45 VR 415 TRX
Spare Goodyear or Michelin 115/80 R 18

Electrical
Battery 12 volt, 66 Ah, AC Delco
Alternator 66 amp, AC Delco
Fuses 24
Headlights Halogen, 110 W on dip, 120 W on main

Dimensions
Wheelbase	100.4 in (255.0 cm)
Front track	59.9 in (151.8 cm)
Rear track	65.4 in (166.0 cm)
Length	176.5 in (448.5 cm)
Width	77.8 in (197.6 cm)
Height	44.5 in (113.0 cm)
Weight	32.28 cwt (1640 kg)
Weight distribution	41.3/587 F/R

Interior
SAE volume, front seat 47 cu ft
SAE volume, boot space 5 cu ft
Headroom 36.0 in (914 cm)
Seats 2 bucket type, 20.0 in (50.8 cm) wide
Squab rake adjustment 45 degrees
Adjustment available Fore and aft, squab, front height

Instrumentation
Instruments fitted 200 mph speedo, 10,000 rpm tacho, six-figure odometer, three-figure plus one decimal place trip odometer, oil pressure gauge, water temperature gauge, oil temperature gauge and fuel gauge
Warning lights Alternator, handbrake, brake system, low fuel, headlights, sidelights, seatbelts, hazard warning lights, mainbeam, indicators, bonnet open, engine cover open, converter overheating, heated rear window

Capacities
Fuel 25.3 gal (115 litre) dual main tanks, 3.9 gal (18 litre) reserve tank
Oil 27 pint (15.5 litre)

Guarantee
Duration UK – 12 months, unlimited mileage
US – 24 months/24,000 miles

Maintenance
Major service 6000 miles
Optional extras
Listed Fitted leather suitcases – £1590.83

IMPORTERS
UK Maranello Concessionaires Ltd., Crabtree Road, Thorpe Industrial Estate, Egham, Surrey TW20 8RJ
US Ferrari North America, 777, Terrace Ave., Hasbrouck Heights, N.J. 07604

WORKING ON THE TESTAROSSA

Ferraris have a pretty awesome reputation when it comes to maintenance. But with such cars regular maintenance is absolutely essential, whatever the cost, and it is likely to be high. Few owners are likely to tackle their own servicing and repair work on a newer Ferrari, though some enthusiasts may do so on older examples.

But what is this Testarossa like to work on? How does it compare with previous models? Is it a practical car from a mechanical standpoint? Has Ferrari quality really improved? To answer these questions, and more, I visited Ferrari specialist Bob Houghton, unquestionably an authority on the technicalities of the marque. Bob began working on Ferraris in the late sixties and has devoted his life to the marque since that time. He was one of the founding members of David Clarke's Graypaul Motors, where he ran the workshops and was in charge of as many as 23 mechanics. After nine years with Graypaul, he left to co-form Rosso Racing and in 1985 he set up on his own in Northleach in Gloucestershire. Apart from servicing and general mechanical work, his company restores Ferraris, he has an engine rebuilding shop, a fabricating section and comprehensive stores, and he prepares Ferraris for most of the big names in historic racing. His client list is about as impressive as the selection of cars one sees in his workshop. On a recent visit I espied a 250GTO, four 512s, Daytonas, a Formula One Dino, a Lusso, a 275GTB/4, a couple of

seventies Formula One cars, and many more. Customers send cars from the States in crates for Houghton and his men to assemble, and they travel from mainland Europe for a service. Not surprisingly he counts a number of Testarossa owners amongst his customers.

'Things have got better since Fiat have been involved. For instance, ten years ago you could have a wiring loom where you traced the wires through, and suddenly they would have soldered a different coloured wire into that loom – this would be at the factory. And so in those days you did have a helluva job to trace anything! Now it is all computerised and the wiring is good. Ferraris, over the last five years, have come on in leaps and bounds.

'In the last three years the bodywork has also become a lot better. The bodywork used to be terrible. I think Ferrari used to spend all their money on the mechanics, and then it was almost as if they used to run out of money at the end, before they put the body on.

'It's a really good car now but between the Daytona, which finished around about 1973/74, and a few years ago, there was a gap. The Boxer was a nice car but they never handled properly – all the weight was in one place and they used to oversteer quite badly if you got into trouble. From the Daytona until five years ago, there was a black hole. They never built what I call real Ferraris, whereas now with the Testarossa and, of course, the 288GTO – and the F40's just another breed! – they're starting to get back to building real Ferraris again. That's my view. The 348, too, is going to be a fantastic car.

'I like a car that's got charisma. For instance, you get into a 328, switch on, it all happens for you, but there is no feel to it – it doesn't feel that this is a real racer. But I suppose Ferrari has to build cars for such a wide market now. They are not all enthusiasts.'

I mentioned to Bob my feelings on driving the Daytona and Testarossa. The former was vibrant and more akin to a competition car. The latter was mightily impressive but .... 'Dull. It is dull. The last of the front-engined Ferraris, the Daytona, is a true Ferrari there's no doubt. But I think the Testarossa is the start of getting back into the groove again. We do one or two mods to Testarossas which actually make them incredible – suspension, brakes, exhaust. It then sounds like a Ferrari, and stops and handles like a Ferrari. A bog-standard TR, I would agree, is a boring car, but when you do a few mods to them you can make them really good. But they couldn't do it at the factory

because it would make them too hard, and too noisy to comply with the Swiss regulations – and all the other different regulations.

'If you spend four grand on a Testarossa you can transform it – not into a racer, but a nice, tweaked, tight car.'

As I began to describe the rather hair-raising experience of the front end moving around under braking, Bob make a weaving motion with his hand before I had even got to the point.

'That's right. We can cure all that. You get a bit of bump-steer with it. It is a bit hairy but that can all be cured.

'The cars are very easy to work on. The only tricky part is setting up the hydrocarbon levels on the injection. Everything else is dead easy. For a big service, for instance, you'd drop the whole engine out underneath, like a Porsche, change the belts and so on, and it makes it very easy to work on. Normally you would do that every 12,000 miles, but you are talking, probably, of every three years.

'Could one do 12,000 a year in a Testarossa?' I asked.

'Oh yes. I've got a Frenchman that literally drives it flat out wherever he goes. He gives it some stick and he drives it every day. He's got flats in Paris and London. He pops over the Channel, we service it and he pops back again. He's not a lunatic but he loves his Ferrari. He says that if he gets caught, he gets caught! He bought a Ferrari to go fast.'

I questioned Bob further on how the Boxer compared with the Testarossa.

'It's like the difference between chalk and cheese. The Boxers are a good car but you get a lot of kick-back from the steering. They don't handle particularly well. They pitch a lot at high speed. The Testarossa is really the Rolls-Royce of the Boxers. They have come on so much and are far more sorted.

'The Testarossa is easier to work on definitely. They are more complicated than a Boxer, but they've made life so much easier.'

As to V12s versus flat-12s, 'I've always loved the V12s, personally. They're no different to work on, there's no difference at all.

'I think the biggest recent mistake that Ferrari have made was to get rid of Forghieri. He was the man – he's probably my idol. He was the engineer. At the moment they've got nobody who was switched on like he was.'

On construction, Bob had this to say, 'Ferrari build

such strong chassis. You don't hear of many people getting killed in a Ferrari. One of my customers hit a lorry with his Boxer, and he almost wrote the lorry off. He got out of it with a broken nose! I don't know about the newer Ferraris, because I haven't seen many Testarossas which have had an accident.'

As to why the bodies rot so badly, 'I don't think the newer ones do, in fact, I know they don't. I think with the older ones it was the way they were made in those days. They all tended to rot around where they had been welded and they weren't really cleaned properly before they were primed and painted. I think that has a lot to do with it, and I don't think the steel they used was as good as it should have been. They are making good bodies now and this ZincroX – we don't know a lot about it yet – seems to be good stuff.

'There have been few production changes since the Testarossa was announced. The changes have been mainly cosmetic ones, like the fitting of a wing mirror on the passenger side, and a few odd things inside the car. Mechanically there has been nothing really that's noticeable.'

Just occasionally, one of Houghton's existing Ferrari customers will manage to persuade him to work on what he terms a 'foreigner', that is a Lamborghini or a Maserati. Admittedly, they are mainly older ones but I thought it relevant to ask him how the engineering compared in his opinion.

'I think Lamborghinis are a bit agricultural, and so are Maseratis. But I am just biased towards Ferraris. After doing a few engine rebuilds, I have noticed a lack of finesse in a lot of things. On the Lamborghini the blocks are quite heavy and they're not nicely polished inside, but left rough. It's almost as if not as much care has been put into building it, like a Ferrari guy would.

'Ferraris have just got so much charisma. Porsches are a nice car, and I've always said a German-built Ferrari would be the best car in the world, but the Germans have got no panache, they're so dull. If you have a Porsche, fine, it's a great car, but if you get out of a Porsche and into a Ferrari you've got so much more happening – the gatechange, the noise. They do break occasionally, though, like all cars, but they are pretty reliable. The automation has helped quality and with modern-day materials and machines they can run tighter tolerances.

'I think it's every man to his own. I don't like anybody knocking Ferraris!'

Autofolio

PHOTO NOTES

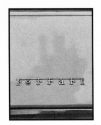

Photographic sessions involving cars are generally reckoned to be glamorous occasions, with 'precious' people fidgeting here and there.

In this case the car itself had undoubted glamorous appeal; the weather, on the other hand, this had anything but. Owner Paul Lennon wasn't fidgeting. He is, however, a most precious person of the best kind; a veritable treasure. Surviving sorties in rain and fog, he finally drove to Brighton when the sun shone, bearing the marks of chicken-pox on all visible skin – and all for the sake of art!

Thanks also to the Weald and Downland Open Air Museum for permission to photograph there, despite continuous heavy rain. Also to two more treasures, John and Lisa, members of staff at the museum and press-ganged models.

The film used throughout the book is Fuji 100 Professional and 400 Professional colour with a sprinkling of the excellent Kodachrome 200. Black and white film was T-MAX 400 (TMY)

The cameras used were a Hasselblad with 50 mm, 80 mm and 150 mm lenses, and Leica R4 with a range of Leica lenses from 16 mm to 560 mm.